FIC   Wood, Phyllis Anderson
WOO   This time count me in

17A1158

DATE			
MAY 7 86			
NOV 20 '90			

THIS TIME COUNT ME IN

A HIWAY BOOK

THIS TIME COUNT ME IN

by

PHYLLIS ANDERSON WOOD

HIWAY

THE WESTMINSTER PRESS

Philadelphia

Book Design by Dorothy Alden Smith

Published by The Westminster Press®
Philadelphia, Pennsylvania

PRINTED IN THE UNITED STATES OF AMERICA
9 8 7 6 5 4 3 2

84-345

Library of Congress Cataloging in Publication Data

Wood, Phyllis Anderson.
    This time count me in.

    "A Hiway book."
    SUMMARY: Peggy's anxieties about her new school fade when she discovers friends among the students in her reading class.
    [1. School stories. 2. Friendship—Fiction]
I. Title.
PZ7.W854Th   [Fic.]   80–15068
ISBN 0-664-32665-X

1

PEGGY CALLED FROM HER BEDROOM. "SEE WHAT the girls are wearing will you, Mom?" Her mother was looking out at the sidewalk.

"Two jeans," Mrs. Marklee reported, "one skirt, eight . . . nine . . . no, better make that eleven pants outfits."

"Ooh no," Peggy groaned. "I blew it already. I thought they'd all be in skirts."

She flew around her room, opening and slamming drawers and muttering to herself. "Shows you how much I know about public high schools. Everything I do is going to be wrong. I just know it."

"Well, I did see one skirt," Mrs. Marklee called back.

"One skirt!" Peggy echoed. "Do you think I want to be the *other* skirt in a school full of pants?"

Peggy finally emerged from her room and walked slowly to the hall mirror and stared into it. Brown hair, squeaky clean. Blue eyes, sort of pale. Figure, so-so.

Completing a full turn, Peggy made a face at the

girl in the mirror. "Yecch. St. Anne's shows all over me."

"You'll be fine, once you get going," her mother told her. "Any new school is hard at first. You knew that when you decided to transfer to Jefferson."

Mrs. Marklee glanced at her daughter, expecting the usual fireworks on that touchy point. Peggy didn't seem to hear. She was gazing at the mirror, her face a blank mask.

Mrs. Marklee picked up Peggy's jacket. "Here you go," she said.

Peggy, sagging like a rag doll, permitted her mother to work the jacket over her limp arms.

"Now this." Mrs. Marklee slid a purse strap over Peggy's drooping shoulder.

"And this." She bent Peggy's right arm and slid in a brand-new binder. "There you are. You look fine. The tan pants and knit top are just right."

Mrs. Marklee turned her daughter and gave her a gentle push. Then she brushed past to open the door.

Woodenly, Peggy inched forward, lifting her feet like lead weights. Step . . . step . . . down . . . down . . . step . . . step . . .

Suddenly the spell broke. Peggy's eyes came to life. Like a frightened animal, she darted back up the steps and into the house.

Huddling on the couch, she tied and untied knots in her purse strap. Mrs. Marklee waited.

"It's insane!" Peggy finally blurted out. "Whatever made me do it?"

"You wanted some friends who weren't all white,"

8

her mother told her. She paused. "And you wanted boys in your classes, too. Remember?"

Peggy smiled weakly. How hard she had worked to get her mother's permission for the transfer. There was nothing more to be said. Pulling herself to her feet, she picked up her binder and walked out the door, waving good-by over her shoulder.

"It will be easier tomorrow," Mrs. Marklee called after her.

Peggy stopped at the sidewalk for a moment to gather her courage. Jefferson High School was only three blocks away, and a wave of students was rolling toward it.

I guess all these people have been doing this right along, Peggy thought. But I never saw them—I left so early to catch the bus to St. Anne's.

Before Peggy reached the corner, the Jefferson warning bell rang. People near her broke into a run. Peggy heard racing feet behind her. She held her breath.

Laughing boys flew by on both sides. Peggy stopped in the middle of the sidewalk, feeling a little scared. The boys hardly noticed her.

After the crowd had passed, a straggler accidentally brushed against Peggy. Jumping, she dropped her binder.

"Oops, sorry," the boy said, skidding to a stop. He dusted off the binder and handed it back, smiling in an open, friendly way. Peggy melted in panic. She couldn't find words to reply.

"You okay?" the boy asked, walking backward as

he waited for an answer. Peggy could feel her cheeks turning pink. She nodded. The boy raised one arm in a salute, then joined his friend in the final dash to school. Peggy was left with her embarrassment.

Brilliant conversation, she told herself. The boys will love you.

She stared ahead at Jefferson High School, sprawled out like some sleeping monster. It looked big and ugly, ready to come alive and eat her.

How will I know where to go? she worried. What do I do during lunch hour? I'll bet I won't even be able to find a girls' rest room. What if nobody speaks to me all day long?

A worse fear surfaced. What if someone does speak to me and I can't answer any better than I did just now?

The sound of more running feet quickly brought Peggy's mind back to the sidewalk. This time she was engulfed by girls.

"Join the late crowd!" one girl called over her shoulder as she passed Peggy. "It's the only way to go."

Peggy was taken off guard. By the time she came up with an answer, the girls were way ahead.

"Dummy!" she said out loud. "What's so hard about laughing with some other girls who are late?"

Scolding herself as she walked, Peggy finally passed through the campus gate. By this time she was really upset. Already she had been a mess with boys and a failure with girls. This left only the adults. Can I do any worse with them? she wondered.

2

PEGGY WAS SURPRISED WHEN THE PEOPLE IN THE office were helpful. After filling out six forms, she was sent to the counseling office.

Peggy's counselor, Mrs. Chan, studied the transcript from St. Anne's. Then she reached for two typed sheets. "Before we program you, Peggy, will you take this quick test of reading skills?"

Peggy tensed up at the idea of a reading test. "I can read," she said.

"I know you can," Mrs. Chan replied. "This is simply to help us place you in the right English class."

Peggy finished the test in fifteen minutes, sensing she had not done well at all. She watched Mrs. Chan count the wrong answers. I knew it, she thought. I knew something would go wrong.

"It would probably be helpful for you to spend some time in our Reading Lab," Mrs. Chan suggested.

"Oh no," Peggy protested. "I want regular English. I'll work."

"Why don't you want Reading Lab?"

"I know the kind of kids they send there."

11

"Our lab is not like that. Lots of our good kids ask to take it."

Peggy was doubtful.

"If it doesn't work out, we'll make a change," Mrs. Chan promised. She wrote "Reading Lab" on Peggy's sheet, then added the other courses Peggy would need.

At last she offered the program for approval. By then Peggy would have agreed to anything. None of it seemed real, anyway.

As Peggy started to leave the office, Mrs. Chan pointed down the hall. "Your first-period class is at the end on the right. You still have time to get signed in."

Peggy stared at the empty hallway and then looked back to Mrs. Chan, who was waiting for some response. "Everything okay?" she asked. "All set?"

Peggy managed a nod. "I think so. Thanks."

Mrs. Chan gave Peggy a friendly smile. "I'll be here. Keep in touch."

Peggy's eyes followed her counselor as she returned to her desk. Then Peggy slowly moved down the hall toward her first-period classroom. Before she reached the room, the passing bell rang. Students poured into the hallway—jostling, shouting, laughing, elbowing their way along. Trembling, Peggy flattened herself against the wall until the passing period was over.

The hallway emptied as quickly as it had filled up.

Peggy looked at her schedule. Second period, P.E. She made a very quick decision. There's no way I'm going to face P.E. on my first day here. I'll spend the period locating my other classes instead. Just so I'll know where they are, that's all.

While she was searching for her science room, Peggy passed the library. An idea hit her. I'll find myself a corner in there where I can study the Jefferson kids for a while. Just to watch them and see how they act.

She sat down at a small table and opened her binder to look busy. She had forgotten—the binder had one hundred blank sheets. No work yet. She hastily closed the binder and reached for the nearest book.

Hidden safely behind *The Gothic Cathedrals of France,* Peggy soon lost touch with time. The people fascinated her. Will they accept me? she worried. I'm such a dummy about so many things.

Peggy didn't notice when one period ended and another period began. Is this third now? Fourth?

Whatever, I've got to find a rest room. Then I'll come back here and watch people again. It'll be a good way to break in. They won't miss me if I haven't signed in.

Peggy found a rest room. In a nervous sort of way she hoped there would be somebody in it. She might try saying "Hi" or something. Pushing the door open, she peered around inside. My luck, she told herself. Nobody but me. Not even someone smoking.

Studying her reflection in the mirror, Peggy decided she really wasn't too far off. Hairstyle? Not bad. Clothes? Nothing to make her stand out too much as a newcomer. On the surface, anyhow. Inside, she felt like a mess.

13

Before Peggy realized the period was ending, the passing bell rang. Girls poured into the rest room. Cornered by the crushing crowd, Peggy could only stand near the wall and look busy combing her hair.

Nobody seemed to notice her. But then again, nobody made fun of her either.

"Got a match?" one girl asked.

"Sorry," Peggy managed to answer.

Trying not to be obvious, Peggy studied the faces in the mirror. Which of these girls will become my friends? she wondered. Any of them?

Peggy especially admired two of the black girls. So sure of themselves. Clothes so right. So good-natured, the way they joked. I'll never be that comfortable, Peggy worried.

The bell rang. The crowd drained away. Peggy was left looking at her own small reflection in the wall-sized mirror. Well, kid, at least you were surrounded by the action for a few minutes, she told herself. And you survived.

Peggy headed down the empty corridor, back toward the library. She had almost reached the library door when an important-looking man passed by. I'll bet he's the principal, she thought.

The man turned back to Peggy. "Don't you belong in some class?"

"Yes." Peggy felt as if the roof were falling in. She had never had a man principal before. And here she was in trouble with this one on the first day—if that's who he was.

"What room should you be in?"

Peggy had to pull out her class schedule to find out.

14

"207?" It came out as a question instead of an answer.

"May I see?"

Peggy handed him the schedule. "New sophomore transfer student. Peggy Marklee. Welcome to Jeff, Peggy. Are you lost?"

"A little." She couldn't very well tell him she had been planning to hide out in the library.

"Come on, I'll show you where 207 is."

Peggy had to hurry to keep up with the man's long stride.

"First room on the left inside this wing," he told her.

"Thank you," Peggy answered, assuming he was leaving her there.

Instead, the man went right to the door of 207 and opened it. Peggy was ready to die.

"Hello, Mr. Burt," the teacher said.

He is the principal, Peggy told herself. I've been hand-delivered to my reading class by the principal!

"This is Peggy Marklee, a new sophomore," Mr. Burt said.

Peggy glanced beyond the teacher, then quickly looked down at the floor. She had seen a sea of faces, all turned toward her.

"Welcome, Peggy. I'm Mrs. Satterlee." The teacher smiled at the principal and closed the door. The room suddenly became very quiet.

Talk about entrances, Peggy thought.

3

PEGGY STOOD NEAR THE DOOR, FEELING AWKWARD and clumsy. How was she ever going to walk across that silent room in front of all those staring people? The nearest empty seat seemed a mile away. She might drop her binder and have to pick up one hundred sheets of paper, with everyone watching. Or she might trip and land flat on her face.

"Peggy, why don't you sit at that front desk over there, just for today," Mrs. Satterlee whispered "I want you to take a couple of tests."

Peggy stared where the teacher had pointed—to one desk, all alone by the side wall. Peggy thought she would die. Anyone sitting there would have a full view of the entire room. Worse still, anyone sitting there could be watched by the whole class. The teacher didn't mean it, Peggy hoped.

Mrs. Satterlee set a test booklet on the desk.

Peggy had no choice. She swallowed hard. Hunching her shoulders and clutching her binder even more tightly, she forged ahead across the room. Like someone caught in a driving storm, she kept her eyes glued to the floor.

The desk was hardly a safe shelter after such a harrowing trip. Sitting there, Peggy felt as if she had a neon sign flashing across her forehead—ST. ANNE'S ACADEMY. On, off, on, off. Everyone staring.

Peggy listened while Mrs. Satterlee explained the tests.

It was hard to think. The idea of everyone looking at her froze her brain. Nothing worked. She couldn't concentrate.

There was no way Peggy could bring herself to look up, not even to count the staring people. They were a threatening blur.

Peggy's only safety was the tests. Forty-five minutes' worth. Frantically, she worked her way through them. When she finished the last question, she set her pen down and rubbed her forehead.

Peering through her fingers, Peggy braved her first glance at the class. Not a soul was looking at her!

Peggy's nervousness about being watched suddenly shifted. She was overcome by a sense of hurt and loneliness instead. I'm here—all the way from St. Anne's—and nobody cares. They don't even know I exist.

Peggy took her hands away from her eyes and openly studied her classmates. In the back right-hand corner of the room she found the two girls she had admired earlier in the rest room. Maybe, with luck, I'll get to know them, Peggy hoped.

In the center rear, a couple of boys caught her eye. They were a strange-looking team. One was tall, handsome, and black, with a jaunty orange knit cap, and a sly look on his face. The other was blond, curly-

17

haired, and pasty-faced. They were exchanging knowing looks and grinning. I'd definitely like to stay away from those guys, Peggy thought.

In the center of the room, near the front, a slim, brown-haired boy with a pleasant face was finishing his work. Peggy couldn't take her eyes off him. Here was exactly what she had left St. Anne's to find.

He doesn't look like one of those big campus heroes or anything, Peggy thought. I wouldn't have a chance with that kind of boy in a million years. But this boy looks just plain nice. I like him.

Somebody nice right in my own class! Peggy marveled. And to think that Mrs. Chan almost had to force me to take Reading Lab. Wow!

Trying to appear casual, Peggy studied each move this boy made, every change in expression. He got up and put his book back on the rack. She admired the way he moved, quiet and sure, tending to his own business.

With my luck he may never even see me, Peggy sighed. He might never speak to me. Oh well, she consoled herself, I can still spend the year watching him.

The bell rang and the boy was gone. The two girls were gone. The guys in the back were gone. Peggy was left sitting at the desk. No one had even noticed that she was there.

"Thank you for completing the test," Mrs. Satterlee said. "It's nice to have you with us."

So glad she noticed, Peggy thought to herself.

It was lunchtime, and the crowd was moving toward the cafeteria. The chance of seeing that boy again, even from a distance, almost lured Peggy to the lunchroom. But going through a cafeteria line alone was not something she felt up to. Instead, she went back to her table in the library to spend the lunch hour safely hidden behind a book.

4

As Mrs. Marklee had said, it did seem easier on the second day. Instead of pants, Peggy confidently put on a skirt. The two girls she had admired in her reading class had worn skirts.

"How come you're leaving so much earlier today?" Mrs. Marklee asked as Peggy picked up her binder and purse and started out the door. "Meeting some new friends?"

"Hardly, Mom," Peggy replied. "Nobody spoke to me yesterday."

Mrs. Marklee was studying her daughter. "Did you see some people who might become friendly after a while?"

Peggy didn't want to be quizzed. She gave her mother a yes-and-no gesture. After all, it was too soon to count on friendships. And then there were the two kids in the back of the room—Peggy didn't even want to think about them. As for that dreamy boy, Peggy wasn't about to discuss him with anyone. She just smiled. "Things are okay, Mom." With a wave she was off.

Peggy wasn't sure where she was off to. School, yes.

But where at school? How could she say she was just going to wander around, hoping to get a glimpse of some boy?

Well, where *do* you get glimpses of boys before school? Peggy wondered as she entered the campus. This had never been a problem at St. Anne's.

Peggy did not forge ahead with her eyes on the ground as she had done on the first day. Instead, she scanned every group she passed. Looking as casual as she could, she moved past crowd after crowd—outside the gym, around the auto shop, near the band room, in the science labs, by the office.

With a sense of panic, Peggy even forced herself to look closely at every girl who was talking with a boy. She would rather not find him at all than find him with another girl, she decided.

When the first warning bell rang, Peggy called off her search in order to go to class. Each period found her stewing over a different worry. Maybe he's not in school today. Maybe he has a steady girl friend. And the worst fear of all—what if he's perfectly free and unattached, but he won't ever look at me? I may be a total nobody to him forever. This devastating possibility carried Peggy into the fourth-period Reading Lab.

As Mrs. Satterlee greeted Peggy, the knot in her stomach eased a bit.

"Let's find you a permanent seat today. How about there, in front of Ron Loftus?" Mrs. Satterlee pointed to the seat directly in front of Peggy's dream.

So his name is Ron! Wow! What luck!

Peggy took her seat just as Ron came into the room

alone. He gathered up his work quietly and sat down behind Peggy. Her feelings ran wild. In nine years at St. Anne's, no Ron had ever sat behind her. Or in front of her. Or even in the same room. Unbelievable!

Should I turn around and say "Hi"? Should I wait till he says something?

The two girls she liked came into the room, and Peggy's thoughts shifted.

"Good morning, Roxanne and Cheryl," Mrs. Satterlee said.

Roxanne and Cheryl, Peggy said to herself. Roxanne must be the tall one. What a beautiful figure! And Cheryl is the heavier one, with a bubbly laugh.

The room was nearly full when the creepy pair arrived.

"Alfred, you owe me a pencil," Mrs. Satterlee reminded the boy in the orange cap.

"Oh. Yeah. Sure. I forgot," he answered. "Gimme a pencil, Walter." He turned to the blond curly-haired kid beside him, who obediently handed over a pencil.

The creeps are called Alfred and Walter, Peggy told herself.

Mrs. Satterlee gave Peggy an assignment for the first week. Wanting to do well, she plunged right into her work. The period flew by.

The bell rang and everyone left. Peggy watched Ron walk out alone. Then she followed the crowd out the door.

Knowing the names of Ron and Roxanne and Cheryl made the class seem more personal, even if nobody spoke to her. Don't hope for any more this soon, she told herself.

Peggy considered following the crowd into the cafeteria. No. Forget that crazy idea. The library would be much safer.

5

THE REST OF THE WEEK MOVED ALONG IN THE SAME pattern. Nobody noticed Peggy. And nobody bothered her. Really it's not that bad, she decided as she walked home on Friday afternoon. Why was I in such a stew the first day?

Peggy flopped on her bed with the telephone. All her close friends from St. Anne's were expecting calls.

"It's really an okay school," she told Monica. "No big hassle at all."

"No," she told Jenny, "it's not a bit creepy having boys in your classes. They're kind of nice, some of them."

"Yeah," she agreed with Karen, "it's fun not wearing a uniform."

"No," she almost snapped back at Judy, "I haven't met any of the boys yet. Come on, it's only been a week. What do you think I am?"

This question had hit a raw nerve. Peggy wasn't about to mention a boy named Ron who happened to sit behind her in fourth period. This information was special. No questions, no jokes, please.

In other years, on weekends, Peggy washed her uniforms. It was a boring job and she hated it.

Now, after her first week at Jeff, Peggy washed everything she owned, just because it was fun. She spent hours before the mirror, matching outfits. She tried every possible combination.

A week ago she had worried about what the other girls would think. Now, whenever she put on an outfit, Peggy found herself wondering how Ron would react. Will it catch Ron's eye? Is this what Ron likes? Will he look at me? Please, will he look at me? And like me!

On Monday, Peggy got up early to allow plenty of time for deciding what to wear. She settled on dark-green pants and a new green-and-blue top. It's kind of showy, Peggy worried as she studied her reflection. A little sexy maybe? Not too much, though . . . I don't think.

Mrs. Marklee marveled as her daughter sailed out the door, forty-five minutes early. She returned Peggy's quick smile and casual wave.

Doggedly, Peggy followed her usual routine, looking for Ron. So far she had never even got a glimpse of him outside of fourth-period class.

Where does that boy keep himself? she kept wondering. Does he drop through a trapdoor in the roof just before Reading Lab each day and exit the same way after class?

When it was time for fourth period, Peggy hung back in the hallway. She figured she might get some kind of clue if she saw which direction Ron came from. This didn't work. A crowd passed in front of Peggy, and when they were gone, Ron had somehow slipped past. There he was, entering 207. Like I said, there's a trapdoor somewhere, she told herself. I'll wait till the very last second. Maybe then he'll look up as I come in. The bell rang. Peggy dashed to the doorway, just making it when the bell stopped. Most of the class were already seated.

Totally lost in her thoughts of Ron, Peggy crossed the room. As she turned to slide into her seat, a wolf whistle came from the back of the room. Then someone let out a long, low "Ooo eee."

Peggy began to burn, her cheeks aflame. It's got to be Alfred and Walter, she told herself. Who else?

Then all the self-doubts began bubbling up inside. It's a put-down. I'm not somebody people would whistle at. Does my new top look all wrong? Is Ron laughing at me, too? I wish I could turn my head to find out.

In her embarrassment, Peggy knocked her binder onto the floor. The pages spilled out. As she leaned down to pick them up, Peggy's head collided with Ron's. He was also reaching for the binder.

"Don't mind them," Ron whispered as he slipped the loose sheets into the binder.

Peggy, completely flustered, took the binder from him and quickly bent over it, trying to look busy.

Her mind was spinning. She realized she hadn't thanked Ron, or answered him, or even looked at him. A voice inside was scolding furiously. Wouldn't you know it? For a whole week you trail some boy

26

and when the perfect moment comes, you blow it. Good going, kid.

Peggy was a mass of regrets. Why didn't I say something clever? Why didn't I smile some kind of winning smile? Why didn't I let my hand touch his as he gave me my binder? Why didn't . . . ? Why didn't . . . ?

Peggy considered turning around to thank Ron. Too late now, she decided. Besides, I'd blush. Everyone would notice. But on the other hand, maybe I should . . .

Peggy's private debate ended abruptly when Mrs. Satterlee handed her an assignment. Gladly she buried herself in the work.

It was hard for Peggy to concentrate when she could feel Alfred and Walter staring at her. She tried to forget them. It didn't help.

Mrs. Satterlee moved around from student to student. Out of the corner of her eye, Peggy kept track of her teacher.

Suddenly a small wad of paper flew past Peggy. It's nothing, she told herself. Someone just missed the wastebasket.

In a moment, another paper wad flew past, this time brushing Peggy's hair. Peggy looked back. Her eyes were drawn to Alfred's bright-orange cap. He was staring out the window. Walter, next to him, was busily writing. Keep calm, she told herself. She turned back to her work.

Almost immediately, a larger ball of paper hit Peggy on the head. I think I'm under attack, she decided. Afraid to look behind again, Peggy stared at the paper ball. Maybe there's a name on it somewhere. No, I shouldn't pick it up. The owner, whoever it is, will be watching.

It was hard to think straight. She could still feel the eyes on her.

In a minute a pencil dropped. Turning toward the sound, Peggy felt a tug at her hair. Out of the corner of her eye she saw Alfred and his bright-orange cap right above her.

"Oops, sorry about this," Alfred said. "I've caught my ring in your hair." Peggy felt him pulling to free it. "I was just on my way to the teacher's desk to leave my work." He set his assignment on Peggy's desk while he worked on his ring.

"Alfred Curtis," Peggy read.

Alfred made a big scene, tugging and pulling. The ring and hair seemed to get more tangled. "I'd hate to have to cut your hair to get my ring loose," he said.

By this time Mrs. Satterlee was standing beside them. "Let me do it, Alfred. Pulling is not the answer. Hold still."

"I'm sorry, Miss." Alfred leaned down. "Miss Whatever-your-name-is."

"This is Peggy," Mrs. Satterlee said as she worked with the tangled hair. "Now, I've freed your ring, Alfred. Will you please go back to your seat."

"I was just going to put my work on your desk."

"I'll take it, Alfred. Thank you."

"I'm sorry, Peggy," Alfred said in a loud whisper as he plopped down in his chair. Then he added for the whole class to hear, "I'll try to stay out of your hair, Peggy."

"That's enough, Alfred," Mrs. Satterlee warned.

The bell for lunch period saved Peggy. The class was out the door before the bell had finished ringing.

"Peggy, I'm sorry about Alfred," Mrs. Satterlee said when they were alone. "He's a handful." She gave a tired sigh and rubbed her neck. "But he doesn't usually get that far out of line."

"It's okay. I'm just not used to being in a class with boys."

"Most boys are not like Alfred. I hope you realize that, Peggy."

"I have some things to learn. That's why I transferred to Jeff."

Peggy left the room and started walking down the hall. She had gone only a few feet when she sensed someone coming up behind. Oh no, she thought, Alfred and Walter weren't waiting behind that door! That idea was too scary. It took Peggy a moment to realize what was really happening.

Ron was beside her, looking right at her with those gray eyes. He had waited for her. He was talking to her.

"Don't let Alfred bother you. He always wants attention."

"He got it, all right."

"Because you're new. As soon as you're old stuff, he'll start on someone else." Ron smiled at Peggy. "Don't worry about it."

They walked along together without talking. Peggy's mind was a three-ring circus. She was on cloud nine. She was in total panic. She was full of wonderful things to say. She was speechless.

"Going to lunch?" Ron asked.

Peggy shook her head. "I have some work to do in the library."

"See you tomorrow, then." Ron quickened his step, turned back to Peggy with a wave, and strode off toward the cafeteria.

Dummy! Peggy yelled to herself. You dummy! You could have gone to lunch with him if only you'd known how to do it right!

Dejectedly, Peggy made her way to the library. Slumped in her seat, she punished herself over and over again. Kid, you deserve to sit here all lunch hour and listen to your stomach growl. That's just exactly what you deserve!

6

ALL AFTERNOON PEGGY ALLOWED HERSELF NO
mercy. She was a mouse in her classes. In the passing
periods she slid along the walls. She made herself
invisible. And then she scolded herself for being such
a creep that no one noticed her.

Peggy left school at three o'clock, totaling up her
failures. It's all over for me at Jeff, she concluded. I
blew my chance with Ron. I might just as well be at
St. Anne's. What good is it to be in classes with boys
if I'm so dumb about talking to them?

Peggy walked slowly through the gate, feeling
thoroughly sorry for herself. And besides, I came
here because I wanted to make some new girl
friends. But who'd want me for a friend?

"Hey," a voice called from behind. "Peggy? Is that
your name?"

Peggy stopped and turned around. Roxanne and
Cheryl were hurrying to catch up.

"Yep, I'm Peggy," she answered shyly. "You're
Roxanne and Cheryl. I heard Mrs. Satterlee say your
names."

"Right."

31

The three of them started walking again.

"How come you never talk to people?" Roxanne asked. "You're always alone. You never speak to anyone in class."

"Nobody knows me," Peggy answered.

"Nobody ever will if you never speak to anybody," Cheryl added.

"I wanted to talk to you, but I never thought you would want to bother with me," Peggy told them. "You're so sure of yourselves. I just feel like a dummy."

"A dummy!" Roxanne was amazed.

"We thought you looked down on our crowd," Cheryl said. "We figured you came from some school you thought was better."

"Better! I came from a school that didn't even have boys."

"Oh no." Cheryl looked at Peggy with pity. "How awful."

"That's how come I don't know much about getting along with boys in class," Peggy began to explain. "Like Alfred . . . I don't know what to do."

Roxanne and Cheryl became serious when Peggy mentioned Alfred's name.

"I'm kind of afraid of him, the way he was acting toward me. I mean, his being black and all, I don't know how to handle it."

Roxanne and Cheryl passed a strange look between them, and Peggy caught it. "I'm sorry. I guess I said the wrong thing. I told you I was a dummy."

"Listen," Roxanne answered, "being black isn't the problem. Alfred would be a bum in any color.

You're afraid of him because he's a hood, not because he's black."

They had reached the corner where Peggy had to turn. "I live down this way," Peggy said. "Thanks for your advice. I know I'm making a lot of mistakes."

"Quit worrying so much," Cheryl told Peggy. "You're doing okay. In fact, you're doing just fine with one boy. I've seen the way Ron watches you."

Peggy's heart leaped all over the place. She was sure the girls could see sparks coming out of her head. But she tried not to show it. She was dying to know more, yet she didn't dare ask.

"Really? What do you know!" Peggy wondered how to sound calm when she was exploding inside. She was so excited she almost took off without saying good-by, but she caught herself. "See you tomorrow."

"Okay. Bye." Cheryl and Roxanne tossed off a friendly wave and went on along the main street.

Peggy floated off down the side street, trying to recapture Cheryl's exact words. *I've seen the way Ron watches you.* That's what she said, isn't it? Is it? Does he really? Was my new top right? Wow!

It was hard to remember how awful she had felt fifteen minutes earlier.

Cheryl's words carried Peggy through the afternoon, the evening, and right on into her dreams.

7

PEGGY WOKE THE NEXT MORNING STILL HAPPY. Uncurling lazily in the bed, she let her arms flop out on each side. Her feet stretched deep into the bedding. She wiggled her toes.

The world's mine today, she thought. A grin spread across her face. Well, not the whole world, maybe. Just Jeff. Well, not all of Jeff, maybe. Just Ron. Well . . . well, maybe he's not mine, really. But at least he knows I'm alive.

Peggy gave up her routine of looking for Ron. I don't need to. He'll be looking at me, she kept thinking. At least that's what Cheryl said.

Peggy fooled along with her breakfast, staring off into space as she sipped her orange juice. She spent ten minutes on her teeth.

Mrs. Marklee was getting edgy. "Are you allowing enough time, dear?"

"Uh-huh."

"Is school going okay?"

"Uh-huh."

"You're later than usual."

"Don't worry. It just takes less time when you know what you're doing."

Mrs. Marklee settled for that.

In a couple of minutes Peggy was off, with a wave and a smile.

Walking alone toward Jeff, she no longer felt any panic when people raced past her. In fact, when the warning bell rang and she was still half a block away, Peggy joined the mad dash. She arrived breathless, feeling very much a part of the action.

Groups were breaking up as people headed for classes. Peggy eyed them casually. She wasn't worrying about Ron. She knew he'd drop through his trapdoor in time for Reading Lab.

He did, appearing out of nowhere when fourth period started. Peggy had already spoken briefly with Roxanne and Cheryl and started her work. Ron moved quietly past and slid into his seat.

Suddenly Peggy realized with panic that her big dreams had been built on what Cheryl thought. But Cheryl doesn't know how I blew it yesterday, not going to lunch with him. He's got to be mad. Or hurt. Or fed up with a know-nothing from private school who can't talk to boys.

On a wild impulse, Peggy turned around and said, "Hi."

Ron looked straight at her. A smile lit his face. "Hi."

Peggy quickly turned back to her work. She knew her cheeks were too pink. Her brain was useless. The big conversation was over.

After the class settled down, Mrs. Satterlee came over and checked Peggy's work. She suggested that Peggy use the answer key at the table.

Peggy walked to the front of the room, wondering if Ron would be looking. Cheryl's words ran through her mind, *I've seen the way Ron watches you.*

Peggy became busy at the front table. Even Alfred and Walter were forgotten for the moment. Peggy was making her last corrections, when a sudden crash jolted her back into the real scene. Someone swore. All eyes turned to the back of the room.

Walter was on the floor. His chair had tipped backward. Making a big thing of picking himself up, he rattled the chair as he set it upright. He rubbed his back slowly, then dropped into his seat.

"You okay, Walt?" Alfred asked dramatically. He had been standing near the teacher's desk when Walter fell. Rushing to the back of the room, he made a loud fuss over his friend's mishap. The two of them exchanged glances and then settled down. Walter buried his face in his book. Alfred stared out the window.

Funny about those two guys, Peggy thought. Walter drops a lot of things—books, pencils, paper—and when Walter drops things, Alfred is usually out of his seat.

Peggy closed the answer book and put it back. She was ready to turn and face the adoring look Cheryl had said would be on Ron's face.

Ron's adoring gaze? Ron, deep in his book, wasn't even watching her.

Go and sit down, Peggy told herself in disgust. She

walked to her desk, her mind all wrapped up in her disappointment.

If Peggy hadn't been dreaming about Ron, she might have sensed trouble sooner. But she was in her seat before she realized what had happened. Her things were gone. She had left them on her desk. Her gold pen, a going-away gift from St. Anne's. Her binder, containing a personal letter from Jenny.

Trying to look casual, Peggy glanced around the room for clues. Walter still had his face in a book. Alfred, as usual, was staring out the window. The other people didn't seem to know Peggy had a problem.

"Did you see my things?" Peggy whispered to Ron. Ron looked up from his work. "What things?"

Peggy motioned for him to forget it. Her eyes were on Alfred. He had started to wander around the room again. He took the long way to the pencil sharpener. He stopped by Mrs. Satterlee's desk, but moved on when she looked up. He idly hung around the correcting table. He turned the bookrack and smiled as it squeaked. He wandered back to the pencil sharpener and broke three pencil points in a row.

Peggy, watching Alfred's act, kept thinking of what the girls had said. *You're afraid of Alfred because he's a hood.* They're right, Peggy decided. There is something sinister in Alfred.

Alfred moved along until he stood beside the bookshelf. He fingered the books idly. "Hey, Peggy," he said out loud, "what's your binder doing on this shelf?"

A yellow paper was hanging out of the binder.

Alfred looked curiously at the paper. "Answer Key— Vocabulary Book Two," he read from the sheet.

"Take your seat, please, Alfred." Mrs. Satterlee walked over and took the binder from his hands.

"This is yours, I believe." She placed the binder on Peggy's desk. "And this is mine," she added as she walked away with the answer key. "And now let's get back to work."

Peggy wished the floor would open up and swallow her. My gold pen, she mourned. I'll never get it back. It's a goner, for sure.

Just then Roxanne slipped Peggy a note. "What else is missing?"

"My gold pen," Peggy scrawled on the scrap of paper. She passed it back.

Roxanne flashed Peggy a "watch this" kind of look. First she glanced around to see where Mrs. Satterlee was. Then she rose quietly from her seat. Like an actress in the wings, about to go onstage, she adjusted her skirt and stood poised. Peggy watched, fascinated.

Walking very slowly, her head high, shoulders square, Roxanne approached Alfred's desk. Alfred looked up, trying to appear cool.

Roxanne stood over him, one hand held out, the other on her hip.

"What's your problem?" Alfred asked in a flip manner.

"Let's have it!"

"Have what?"

Roxanne slapped down her hand on Alfred's desk, palm up, waiting. "The gold pen. What else!"

38

"What are you talking about, girl?"

"Give me that pen, Alfred! Right now!" Roxanne's eyes were flashing. Her tone was angry.

Slowly, Alfred pulled the pen from his pocket and laid it in Roxanne's hand. Her fingers closed around it. She raised the pen to the level of Alfred's face and waved it threateningly at him. "So help me, if you ever bother that girl again, you'll have to deal with us. She's our friend. Hear?"

Wow, that's what I call class, Peggy was saying to herself.

Carefully casual, Roxanne sauntered over and laid the gold pen on Peggy's desk. Peggy grinned up at her. "Thanks, Roxanne," she whispered. "Thanks a lot."

Roxanne shrugged her shoulders as if to say it was nothing. She broke into a broad smile just as the bell rang. With a wave to Peggy, she was swept out the door by Cheryl's bubbling chatter.

Peggy stayed in her seat, wanting to explain things to Mrs. Satterlee. Ron kept reading his book.

"Is the book that absorbing?" Mrs. Satterlee asked. Ron glanced around to be sure he and Peggy were alone with the teacher.

He ignored the question. "Don't blame Peggy for taking that answer key, Mrs. Satterlee. She didn't do it."

"I know, Ron. Alfred planted it there. But thank you for protecting Peggy."

"Then you know what's going on?"

Mrs. Satterlee nodded. "I was going to deal with Alfred when he didn't have an audience. I'm trying to give him every possible chance, since he's on probation. But I suspect it's only a matter of time before he's in real trouble."

Peggy glanced up at Ron. "Thanks, you were nice to stick around to help."

"That's okay," Ron replied. A blush was creeping up his cheeks. "Just don't let Alfred get to you."

"I'm trying not to, but what's coming next?"

"With Alfred, who knows!" Ron shrugged as he headed for the door.

Peggy waved at Mrs. Satterlee. Then she followed Ron into the hall.

8

RON AND PEGGY WALKED SLOWLY DOWN THE COR-
ridor, empty now except for a few stragglers.

"Where are you going to eat?" Ron asked, breaking the silence.

"I don't know." The answer sounded dumb.

"Do you usually eat in the cafeteria?"

"I haven't been eating lunch."

"Dieting?"

"No. I just haven't been hungry at noontime."

Ron looked at Peggy. She felt him seeing right
through her.

"That's not really true," Peggy confessed. "But the
truth is too corny to tell you."

"Try me."

"I was afraid to go alone to the cafeteria." Peggy
looked shyly at Ron, expecting him to laugh.

"Well! Let's take care of that right now." Ron
quickened his pace. Peggy followed along.

"There are two lines," Ron pointed out as they
entered the cafeteria. "The quick sandwich and milk
line, or the hot lunch line. Take your choice."

41

"Hot lunch," Peggy answered quickly. "It's probably more complicated to learn."

"Not really," Ron laughed. "A monkey could make it through alone after the first time."

"Well, you go first," Peggy suggested. "The monkey can follow you."

The mental image of Ron leading his monkey through the food line struck them both at the same moment. A giggle started and then grew. Soon they were laughing so hard that the boy behind Peggy handed her some silverware and pointed toward the moving line.

Any other time Peggy would have died of embarrassment. This time, with Ron sharing the laugh, Peggy smiled openly at the boy and then followed Ron through the hot lunch service.

Ron spotted a couple of seats together at one of the tables and led the way to them.

"Now that didn't take any great talent, did it?" he asked when they were seated.

Peggy shook her head, feeling a little silly about being afraid to tackle it alone.

"But I know how you feel. I'm pretty new, myself."

"You're new to Jeff?" Peggy couldn't believe it. "I thought you'd been here for a couple of years."

"Only one month before school closed last June. That's all I've been at Jeff before this semester," Ron told her. "My dad works for the Forest Service. He got transferred down here three weeks before finals. I finished off my freshman year here. But barely."

Peggy was studying Ron, trying to imagine where he had been before Jeff. So far she had guessed wrong on all counts. "Where did you come from?" she asked.

"Way up in the mountains. A little town with a high school of one hundred kids. Five teachers."

"You came from a little school, too?" Peggy's delight made Ron smile. "So did I. St. Anne's Academy. All girls."

"Why did you change?" Ron asked. "Your folks move?"

Don't tell him it was to meet boys, Peggy warned herself. Try to be a little smart for once. She shrugged her shoulders. "It seemed like a good idea to go to public school. Meet new people. Learn different things."

"Have you met new people?"

"I don't seem to be very good at it yet," Peggy confessed. "It'll take a while, I guess."

Ron smiled in a knowing way.

"How did you get into things so quickly?" Peggy asked.

"I'm not in," Ron replied. "I really haven't made any friends here yet."

Peggy shot him a surprised glance.

"Except you," he added quickly, looking embarrassed. "But I don't mind. I've always been kind of a loner."

"I like Cheryl and Roxanne," Peggy said. "They've been nice to me."

"Yeah, they—hey, here they come now."

Peggy turned to look. Roxanne and Cheryl were coming toward them. Their pathway was paved with friends. Waving. Smiling. Calling.

Roxanne and Cheryl sat down across from Peggy and Ron and leaned forward to talk.

"We saw you both stay after class," Cheryl said, "so we figured you were setting Mrs. Satterlee straight. What happened?"

"She had it straight already," Ron replied. "We didn't tell her anything she didn't know."

"Then why didn't she do something?" Roxanne asked.

"She will—without the class watching."

"Hey, thanks a lot for your help," Peggy told the girls.

"We were just lucky," Cheryl said. "We looked up at the right moment to see what he did."

The fifth-period warning bell rang. With a wave, Roxanne and Cheryl sailed off. Peggy watched them go, admiring their sureness.

"Thanks for feeding the monkey," Peggy told Ron.

"Anytime," he replied.

Peggy looked at the clock in horror. "Oh no, I'm going to be late for fifth period. See you."

Before she realized what she was doing, Peggy was flying down the hall to fifth period. Not tiptoeing. Not sticking close to the walls. She was racing down the corridor, dodging bodies and books as if she had been doing it at Jeff for years.

9

Peggy went home that day knowing things had changed. On the surface nothing was different. Ron didn't ask her for a date. Cheryl and Roxanne didn't invite her to have a milk shake with them. But Peggy felt different about herself. She had managed to survive one of Alfred's plots. And she knew people who would help her.

Little by little, day by day, Peggy began to be more at ease with her new friends. She turned and whispered a comment to one of them in Reading Lab. She caught up with the girls or Ron in the hallway and talked as they walked. And, best of all, Ron continued to eat with her in the cafeteria. Things were coming together for Peggy at Jeff.

One day at lunch Ron said, "You're different these days. You know that? More comfortable or something."

Peggy smiled. She had just been thinking the same thing.

"Even Alfred has been leaving you alone," Ron pointed out. "Maybe your initiation is over."

"I hope that doesn't mean I'm in his club now."

Peggy always felt uneasy when she thought of Alfred. She sat silently, studying her sandwich.

Ron wished he hadn't brought up the subject. "Here, have a cookie. They're pretty good today." He handed Peggy one of his chocolate chip cookies.

Looking up, Peggy found Ron staring intently at her. She began to melt inside. No boy had ever looked at her that way before. She felt a new kind of shivery excitement.

Seconds later—or minutes, maybe—Peggy realized that the cookie was still there. She couldn't tell how long Ron had been holding it out to her. Her time clock had stopped.

Peggy accepted the cookie, hoping her hand might brush Ron's as she took it. But eat that cookie? How could she possibly eat the first gift a boy had given her since she was ten? You're supposed to keep such things forever, like a flower pressed in an album. A pressed cookie? Peggy grinned.

"That's better." Ron smiled at Peggy's smile. She melted all over again.

Ron didn't seem to know that Peggy was all loose pieces inside. He couldn't see that her brain was like jelly. As if nothing at all had happened, he simply picked up the trash and took it to a garbage can. "Guess we'd better get to fifth period."

Peggy forced her brain to think straight. She dared herself to talk sense as Ron walked with her to her math class. But her math teacher couldn't stop her dreaming. And her science teacher couldn't bring her down to earth.

Peggy rode her little pink cloud home and parked

46

it near her bed where she could board it as she dropped off to sleep.

She hadn't really come off it by morning.

Before her mother was up, Peggy was floating dreamily around the kitchen, fixing eggs and toast and juice. When Mrs. Marklee came in to make her own breakfast, Peggy glanced up, hardly aware of her mother's presence.

Mrs. Marklee was uneasy about her daughter, who seemed miles away. "You're not talking much these days."

Peggy looked up, surprised. She had been carrying on non-stop conversations inside her head. She hadn't realized how little she was saying out loud.

"Anything wrong?" her mother asked. "You went right to your room after school yesterday. You were silent at dinner. And all evening you were in your room again. I'm worried about you."

"No need to worry, Mom." Peggy searched for some explanation. "I just had a lot of reading to do for a class."

"For your Reading Lab?"

"Uh-huh." Peggy had barely heard the question. She was thinking about Ron.

"I'm glad it's turning out to be a good class." Mrs. Marklee sensed they weren't really talking about the Reading Lab at all.

Peggy felt she should reassure her mother in some way. "It's really okay. There are some nice people in it."

Silence settled over the table again.

47

10

FOR A WHILE AFTER THAT, MEALTIMES BECAME BAD
times for Peggy and her mother.

"You're letting yourself drift into a fantasy world,"
Mrs. Marklee warned Peggy whenever her silences
seemed too long or too frequent.

"Leave me alone," Peggy would always snap back.

"Why can't we talk these days?" her mother would
ask. "Like we used to."

"We're talking," was Peggy's answer.

Then they would withdraw into their own worlds.
Tension would settle over the meal.

After one of these sessions, Peggy sat alone at the
table feeling guilty. Actually, Mom's right, she had to
admit to herself. I really am creating a lot of dreams
that don't match up with the real-life facts.

Like lunchtime with Ron. We talk about classes
and school. But we never get beyond that—to him
and me and us. Not like we do in my dreams.

In spite of these warnings to herself, Peggy went
right ahead building a whole fantasy world around
Ron. In the daytime her mind ground out the
dreams. Things she and Ron would someday do to-

gether. Secrets they would share. And at night she would go to sleep acting out her dreams of the day.

One morning after a week of this, Peggy entered the campus, aglow with plans. We could go skating in the park. Boating on the lake. Hiking in the hills. And that new amusement park, I'd love to go there.

The dream machine ground on and on. Whoa, Peggy finally shouted to her mind. That's enough. That's too much. She stopped abruptly. For the first time in a week, Peggy started to take a long, hard look at things.

You know what, kid? You really don't know anything about this dreamboat of yours.

Think about it. You don't know what he likes to do, what he feels, what he thinks about. You've just made plans for the next five years, and you don't know if he can drive. Or if his folks even have a car.

Again, Peggy tried to let go of the daydreams. He only likes me as cafeteria company, she told herself. I'm not sexy, or even much fun.

But something inside still clung to the dream. We could walk . . . take a bus . . . double-date.

Peggy was so busy protecting her fantasies that she almost walked right past Ron without seeing him. Luckily, something clicked inside. She did a double take.

It was true. There he was, sitting in the courtyard, huddled over a book.

With her dreams still fresh in her mind, Peggy approached Ron. She was certain he would look up any moment and be absolutely delighted to see her.

But Ron was totally unaware of Peggy's plans for him. He was even unaware of her presence.

Peggy, moving up close, looked over the top of his head to see what he was reading. Motor Vehicle Code, she read to herself.

Ron still hadn't noticed her. After the attention she'd been getting in her dreams, it was hard to be ignored.

What do I have to do to get this guy to see me? Peggy wondered. Be a car?

She waved a hand back and forth like a fan before his eyes.

At last she asked, "How come you didn't drop down through your trapdoor like you usually do just in time for fourth period?"

Ron looked up, surprised and confused. "Oh . . . hi." He put a finger on the page to mark his place. "What did you just ask?"

Peggy knew when she asked it that the question would make no sense to him. But he had just messed up all her dreams, and she wanted him to feel stupid.

"Oh, it's just an 'in' joke. Forget it." Peggy wanted Ron to beg for an explanation.

"Okay," Ron replied. He returned to his place in the book.

Peggy was steaming. She started to leave. No! That wasn't what she wanted, either. Do something with this mess, she warned herself frantically. You're blowing it. Forget the dream stuff. Deal with the real boy. And fast!

Using a different approach, Peggy leaned over to see Ron's book. "Getting your learner's permit?"

"Yeah. It's crazy." At last Ron was looking at her. "Up in the mountains I was driving at the age of twelve. But down here my dad won't let me touch the car without a license. So, today I'm going to take the written test for my permit, and then on my sixteenth birthday I can get my license. I don't want to wait even one day longer than I have to."

"What's the big hurry?" Peggy asked. "Why are you so anxious to drive?" She tossed this one out, expecting Ron to follow the script of her daydreams. His answer could only be "To take you out, Peggy."

Ron replied without hesitation. "To go fishing."

To go fishing. Fishing! Peggy repeated the word to herself with distaste.

She was desolate. What about all my plans? she wondered.

Ron flipped the pages of the book. Peggy felt completely left out. Here she had finally found Ron before school and he wasn't a bit interested in talking to her.

"Passing over a double line," Ron mumbled. "Here . . . here it is."

"I'll see you later." Peggy started to move away, still hoping Ron would warm up.

"Okay," he answered without looking up.

Well, Peggy muttered to herself as she walked off, that was a warm and wonderful meeting.

The whole morning went by slightly off tone. Yesterday was so good. Today everything goes thud, Peggy kept thinking.

At the start of fourth period, Peggy acted very busy when Ron entered the room. If he doesn't want to talk to me, then I won't be sitting here looking eager, she told herself.

"Hi, Peg," Ron said as he passed her desk.

Peggy's plans to act cool fell apart. This was the first time Ron ever called her Peg. It seemed close and personal.

"Still studying the code?" she asked.

"Yep," Ron replied.

At last Peggy's brains were coming to her rescue. This time, a practical plan began to take shape in her mind. If she couldn't fight Ron's cars, then why not join them? "I could test you at lunchtime," she suggested.

Ron's face lit up. "Will you? That'll be great. Thanks, Peg."

Peggy sat there, amazed. It was so simple! As she waited impatiently for the period to end, she reviewed what had just happened. Look at it this way, she told herself. Maybe it's not that you're so dumb. You're learning.

11

JUST BEFORE THE BELL RANG, PEGGY BEGAN TO
feel fluttery inside. The way Ron had called her Peg,
and the fact that they were sharing his driver's test
preparation made lunchtime seem much more personal this time.

"Want to walk down Mission Street to The Hamburger Hut?" Ron asked after the bell rang. "You can
test me as we walk."

"Sure," Peggy agreed.

"You can put your things in my locker so you don't
have to carry them."

"Okay."

When they stopped at the locker, Peggy had a
funny, excited feeling. She had never shared a locker
with a boy. Ron took her books and stacked them on
his. "Why not leave your jacket, too?"

Peggy was surprised at how neatly he folded it.
Where did I ever get these funny ideas? she wondered. Just because he's a boy, what did I expect?
Wadded up clothes and a locker plastered with *Play-
boy* centerfolds?

Ron closed the locker and handed Peggy the Vehicle Code. "Let's start with the review questions."

Peggy listened carefully. She wasn't about to let any wrong answers slip by. He's got to pass, she told herself. It's very important to him. To us!

They finished the last review question as they reached The Hamburger Hut.

"No more testing now," Ron said. He stuck the booklet in his pocket. "Thanks a lot."

Peggy smiled. "Sure."

They placed their orders and stood around, waiting for their food. By the time their burgers and shakes were ready, the outdoor tables were full.

"There's a bench across the parking lot," Peggy pointed out.

"Good. Let's get it."

They hurried over to the bench and set their cardboard trays between them.

Peggy leaned back and sighed comfortably. "The sun feels good, doesn't it?"

Ron, freed for the moment from his test preparation, smiled in a relaxed way.

Only then did they realize that a small crowd had gathered right behind their bench. Voices were rising in excitement. Peggy and Ron listened.

"Someone knocked over a garbage can," one woman was telling the others in a shaky voice. "It was a tall young man with blond wavy hair. He seemed embarrassed to have had such an accident."

"But you?" someone asked. "What happened to you?"

"It happened so fast. I'm not sure. I think another young man bumped into me. I lost my balance and almost fell. When I started to get up, my purse was gone."

Ron and Peggy exchanged quick glances.

"Any description of the person who ran into you?" a man asked.

"He was black. And wore an orange cap."

Peggy and Ron dropped their burgers in their laps and stared at each other, stunned.

"Alfred and Walter," Peggy whispered to Ron.

"A smooth act," he whispered back. "Really smooth."

They turned back to their half-eaten burgers.

"I can't eat any more," Peggy said. "The bun tastes like cardboard."

Ron was having trouble choking his food down.

"What should we do?" Peggy asked softly. "Tell the police who it is?"

Ron felt doubtful. "We didn't actually witness anything, Peg. We can't say it's Alfred and Walter just because the lady's description fits some guys we know."

"But we can't let them keep doing this to people, either," Peggy argued. She had strong feelings for this new victim, having been a victim herself, earlier.

"I know," Ron agreed. "But Alfred doesn't wear the only orange cap in town. And the world is full of curly-haired blond kids. Suppose they were picked up by the police on our word, and then they were innocent."

Peggy was trying to work it all through in her mind. "Mrs. Satterlee did say it was just a matter of time," she said.

"Maybe the police are on their trail right now," Ron suggested.

"I don't see even one officer."

Peggy and Ron didn't have much to say as they walked back to school. Even the warm day couldn't lift the chill that had settled in. Walter and Alfred had a way of hanging over people like a dark cloud.

When they reached Ron's locker, Ron took out Peggy's jacket. "Carrying it or wearing it?"

"Think I'll wear it."

Ron held the jacket while Peggy slipped her arms into it. No boy had ever held a coat for her before. Suddenly she was warm all over.

Who needs a jacket on a lovely sunny day? Peggy wondered. But I'm not going to take it off after Ron put it on for me, that's for sure.

Once again her mind was full of Ron, and the idea of their doing things together.

"Listen, don't worry about those two guys," Ron said. "If you want to do some worrying, then worry about my driver's test."

"I'm going to worry all afternoon," Peggy told him. "Until I hear you passed. Do you want to call me when it's over? So I can stop worrying?"

"Sure." Ron scribbled Peggy's number on his book. "So, wish me luck." He flashed her a quick grin.

"You know how to drive," Peggy answered. "But good luck anyhow."

The incident at The Hamburger Hut was pushed to the back of Peggy's mind. And yet, Alfred lurked like an evil shadow there.

12

ALL AFTERNOON PEGGY'S EYES WERE ON THE clock, her mind on Ron.

The minute school was out she rushed home to be near the phone. Curled up on the couch with her homework and a snack, she let her thoughts drift.

He's taking the test now. Pass it, Ron. Please. What do you do when the lights are flashing on a school bus? You can cross over a double line if . . . What does it mean when . . .

The afternoon dragged on into dinner time. He's not going to call, Peggy decided glumly. He's out driving around. He's picking up some girl.

Oh, quit being stupid, she told herself. With a permit he can only use the car with an adult along. He can't carry on a very heavy social life.

When the phone finally did ring at six thirty, Peggy was past hoping. She picked it up very casually. Probably it was a business call for her mother.

"Hello?" Her cheeks quickly flushed as she heard Ron's voice. "Did you pass?" A relieved smile spread across her face. "Of course . . . I'd love to. Hang on. Let me check with Mom."

Peggy sailed into the den, where her mother was typing. "Is it okay if I go out with a friend for a little while?"

Her mother looked up. "Oh? I'm glad you've found someone. What's her name?"

"Ron."

Mrs. Marklee tried to cover her surprise. "Remember, it's a school night."

"I know. It's only to drive his mother over to her sister's house out near the Point."

"Sounds fine. Of course you may."

Peggy whirled to hurry back to the phone.

"I'd like to meet Ron when he comes," her mother called.

"Sure." Peggy picked up the phone. "I can go, Ron . . . Twenty minutes? . . . Sure. That's fine."

It was all happening so fast. So unexpectedly. Her first date—if it was a date—and she didn't even have time to get scared.

Well, it's not such a big date, with his mother along, Peggy thought. But after St. Anne's, anything's big!

Peggy quickly checked her closet. Gray pants and rose top? No, too dressy. Brown pants and striped top? Not right. Jeans and checked shirt? That's better. Don't want to look as if I'm making it a big deal.

Peggy was brushing her hair when her mother appeared in the doorway. "You didn't mention that you had become friends with a boy."

"I know. I was afraid it might go away if I talked about it. I wasn't sure Ron even cared if I was around."

"Apparently he does."

A knock on the door made Peggy drop the hairbrush. For a moment she froze, staring in the mirror. Then she grabbed her jacket and hurried to the door.

Mrs. Marklee stood in the background as Peggy greeted Ron. Then Peggy turned to her. "This is Ron Loftus, Mom."

"I'm glad to know you, Ron." Mrs. Marklee stepped forward and shook his hand. "You're a new driver as of today, I hear."

"Not really," Ron told her. "I've driven since I was twelve, but that was up in the mountains. Down here I have to be legal." He chuckled. "As of today I have a permit to learn."

"Some things get all mixed up, don't they?" Mrs. Marklee said, laughing.

As Peggy and Ron moved toward the car, Ron's mother opened the window and waved to Mrs. Marklee. Peggy felt a quick flash of pride in her mother. She was acting casual, as if boys often came to the house.

Oh, oh, this is going to be something, Peggy thought as she neared the car door. Look at that. Ron's mother sitting between us on our first date. What a laugh that would get at St. Anne's.

But when Ron opened the door, his mother said, "I'll let you slip in first, Peggy. Then I can get out easily at Elaine's."

Mrs. Loftus kept the conversation going all the way out to her sister's house. Peggy had no chance to ask about the driver's test. What is this? she thought. A first date with somebody's mother?

Ron pulled into his aunt's driveway and turned off the engine.

"Can you kids take care of an hour?" Mrs. Loftus asked. "I'll visit with Elaine till eight o'clock. Okay?"

"Sure," Ron told her.

"Watch the time, though," she warned.

"Don't worry."

Mrs. Loftus entered the house. Peggy and Ron were alone.

A wave of panic swept over Peggy. What do you talk about with a boy? Alone.

Ron was running his finger around and around the steering wheel. Am I supposed to start the conversation? Peggy wondered. Why is he so quiet?

Ron looked at his watch. "Want to walk?"

"Sure," Peggy answered. "I've never seen this area."

"You haven't?" Ron seemed to find that hard to believe. "How long have you lived here?"

"All my life."

"And you've never been out here?"

"Believe it or not."

"Your parents don't have a car, then."

"I only have my mother. My parents were divorced years ago. And Mom doesn't need a car to go to work, because she types transcripts at home for court reporters. I've only been where buses go."

"Wow. I'd die if I couldn't get out to places like the Point," Ron said. "Come on. Let me show you."

Forgetting how uneasy she had felt moments earlier, Peggy opened the car door and got out.

"First you have to smell the air," Ron told her.

Peggy breathed deeply. "It's different."

"You're only two blocks from the ocean, that's why."

"I didn't know we were that close."

"We are. Just beyond that row of houses we'll be on the cliffs directly above the water. And see those trees up there about a half a mile away? That's the Point, where there used to be a warning light for ships."

"Must be a good view," Peggy said.

"Fantastic. Let's go."

They cut behind the houses on a footpath, and suddenly it all opened up before them. Waves crashing on the mossy rocks below. Roll upon roll of breakers, chasing each other toward shore.

Peggy tried to sort out her spinning feelings. A shiver ran down her spine.

"It's so new to me," she told Ron. "The whole outdoors. Look at it. I'm fifteen years old, and I'm just starting to learn about all this. I don't know where to begin."

"With the basics," Ron replied cheerfully. "Starting on page one . . ." He opened an imaginary primer and read to Peggy. "This is the ocean." He looked up and swept the seascape with his arms. "This is Ron." He looked at Peggy and pointed to himself. "Ron loves the ocean." Now his reading was flowing along. "See Ron. See the ocean. Ron is a fisherman. Fish, Ron, fish."

By then, Peggy was doubled up with laughter.

"Seriously," Ron said, "fishing's built into my nature. If I can't get to a mountain stream, then I have

61

to get to the ocean to fish. In the city I'm only half alive."

"I had no idea what I was missing." In her mind, Peggy was trying to decide how much of her good feeling was coming from the cliffs and the ocean, and how much was from being with Ron.

"It gets better," Ron told her. He led the way up a narrow path. Peggy followed, now and then picking a stray wild flower. By the time they reached the Point, she had six different kinds. They sat on the ground facing the open sea, leaning against a weather-beaten fallen cypress tree.

Peggy spread out her six flowers. Ron pointed to each one in turn, telling Peggy something about it. "That one I've never seen before," he said. "I'll have to ask my dad about that one." Then he looked at Peggy. "You're not supposed to pick the poppies, though. They're protected by law, you know."

"Dumb me. I didn't know," Peggy replied. "You going to turn me in?"

"Yeah," Ron answered with a wicked grin. He clenched his fist and brought it down lightly on Peggy's knee.

Without thinking, Peggy laid her hand on top of Ron's. If she had planned it ahead of time, she would have dissolved in uncertainty. She hadn't touched a boy since her sandbox days. But with Ron it seemed perfectly natural. How could people share a spot like the Point without touching?

Peggy had a million things to ask Ron. She had trouble picking one to start with.

"Tell me more about your dad's job," she suggested as a starter.

Ron told Peggy about his dad's work with the Forest Service, and she could sense how much of Ron's life, too, belonged to the outdoor world. No wonder a car matters so much to him. Without wheels, how could he even get to the place where his life begins?

"Did you have any trouble with the driver's test?" Peggy asked.

Ron brushed the test off with one quick gesture. "Child's play."

Then Peggy brought up the shadow that had been lurking in the back of her mind. "Have you thought any more about Alfred and Walter?"

"Those two are bad news," Ron replied. "But I think we'll have to let them surface again." He seemed to want to get away from the subject. It was changing the relaxed feeling they had been enjoying.

Ron looked at his watch. "I'm afraid we'd better start back, Peg."

Why does it have to end? Peggy mourned to herself. She stood up and dusted off her jeans. Why couldn't we talk on and on?

Twilight was turning to darkness as they started down the path. Ron led the way, now and then warning Peggy of hazards. "There's a big rock here . . . Watch this root."

I wish he wouldn't let go, Peggy thought as Ron reached back to take her hand at a rough stretch.

When they finally reached the pavement, the whole scene began to seem unreal to Peggy. Was it less than an hour ago that they had sat in the car—Ron running his finger nervously around the steering wheel, she wondering how to start a conversation?

When they got to the car, Ron looked at his watch. "Five minutes to spare." They slid in and closed the doors.

As they sat in silence, Peggy tried to hide a shiver. Ron sensed it.

"Cold?" He started to reach his arm over as if to pull Peggy closer. He stopped and rested his hand on the seat behind her, instead.

The next moment Mrs. Loftus was in the car, waving to her sister and the children.

Peggy tried to keep the magic spell from vanishing. But in the midst of Mrs. Loftus' chatter, it was hard to keep quiet moments alive.

When they reached Peggy's home, Ron let her out on his side and walked with her up the steps.

"I hope you enjoyed tonight," he said without looking at Peggy. "I know I did."

"I loved it."

Ron dug his toe into the doormat, his eyes following the tapping movement of his foot. "I have to confess one thing," he went on, almost in a whisper. "I never took a girl out before. I'm not very smooth and polished."

"Smooth and polished!" Peggy laughed. "Remember me? St. Anne's all the way? Don't ever apologize to me."

Ron grinned. Then he turned and took the stairs two at a time. At the car door he waved. "See you."

"Good night, Peggy," Mrs. Loftus called from the car window.

Peggy waved and went inside. "I'm home, Mom," she called to her mother in the den.

"Have a good time?"

"Uh-huh. We hiked out to the Point while Ron's mother visited her sister."

"Beautiful view from there?"

"Fantastic." Peggy didn't want to talk about it. She wanted to get into bed and relive the evening. "Good night."

Peggy hurried on into her room, got ready for bed, turned off the light, and slipped between the smooth sheets. Then her thoughts about the evening began to float free. The images danced around in her mind, now this picture, now that one—a kaleidoscope of feelings that meant a new way of caring about someone.

13

PEGGY AWOKE THE NEXT MORNING STILL UNDER A magic spell. Humming softly, she took a yellow-flowered blouse from the closet and tried it with brown pants. No, she decided, this isn't a pants day. She slipped into her brick-colored skirt and twirled before the mirror. That's better. Hope Ron likes it.

Suddenly, a twinge of longing passed over Peggy. At St. Anne's, all my friends would have been buzzing around today. I would have been the center of everything. Where did you go? What did he do? How did you feel? What was it like?

Peggy stopped short in her thinking. Wrong. All wrong. I wouldn't talk about last night, anyway. Not to them or to anyone. That evening belongs to Ron and me, not to a bunch of giggling girls.

Still humming, Peggy went into the kitchen. Her mother looked up from reading her typing and smiled. "It's a good morning, I gather."

"Uh-huh." Peggy opened the morning newspaper. Mrs. Marklee could tell there would not be any conversation about Ron.

Behind the paper, Peggy let her mind race ahead

—to school . . . to seeing Roxanne and Cheryl . . . to Ron. Four long hours until fourth period.

Peggy looked in all the likely spots when she reached the campus, but Ron wasn't around. Neither were Cheryl and Roxanne. She did get a glimpse of Alfred and Walter as they disappeared around the back of the gym. Alfred led the way. Walter, a few steps behind, kept looking back to see if he was being followed. He was. A minute later, Mr. Lipman, the vice-principal, strolled along the same route, trying to look casual.

The episode at The Hamburger Hut suddenly came back to Peggy's mind, an unsettling memory that stayed with her for most of the morning.

She arrived early for fourth period, but when she saw Alfred and Walter going into the Reading Lab, she waited in the hallway for Ron or Cheryl and Roxanne.

The girls arrived first. I wonder if they'll know about last night, Peggy thought. Does it show? Do I look super happy or anything?

"Come on in and learn to read," Cheryl said, pulling Peggy into the room.

Ron, arriving with the bell, added a friendly shove. Surrounded by her friends, Peggy quickly forgot about Alfred and Walter.

When Mrs. Satterlee began moving around the room to check homework assignments, Alfred started wandering. He went to the window, the bookshelves, the correcting table. Peggy watched him, fascinated. Alfred was putting on a show. He sharpened his pencil three times, then broke the point twice while testing it. He went to the teacher's desk, making a big thing out of getting a paper clip.

While Alfred was dramatically closing up the clip box, Walter, in the back of the room, started to cough. The coughing became worse. Everyone looked around. Everyone except Peggy. She was learning. When Walter started his scene, Peggy kept her eyes on Alfred.

Quickly and silently, Alfred slid open the teacher's lower desk drawer. He reached down. As he straightened up, Peggy saw him slip something inside his jacket. Her heart sank. She knew she had just witnessed something terrible. Alfred put on his innocent look and walked quickly to his seat to hover over his stricken friend. Walter made a miraculous recovery.

When the period was half over, the intercom phone rang. Mrs. Satterlee answered it.

"The attendance office wants to see you," she told Alfred. He left the room quietly.

In a few minutes the phone rang again. Mrs. Satterlee listened intently. "Hold on, I'll check." She went to the desk and opened the bottom drawer. Returning to the phone, she said, "It's gone. It was here at the beginning of this period. I know that for sure."

Peggy knew she was in on something.

Mrs. Satterlee was still on the phone. "Alfred Curtis is the only person who has left the room this period. He went out when the attendance office called." She listened some more, then hung up the phone.

Mrs. Satterlee sat down at her desk. Her face was

troubled. Several times she opened and closed the desk drawer.

The other students didn't seem to sense what had happened. Only Peggy knew a terrible secret. And she wished she didn't.

Fourth period seemed endless. Peggy felt so alone. If only she could share her secret with Ron, or Roxanne and Cheryl. She couldn't though. Not while Walter was around to carry the word to Alfred.

At last the bell rang.

"See you," Roxanne said with a friendly tap on Peggy's arm as she passed.

Ron waited near the door. Peggy motioned for him to come back in and close the door.

"Mrs. Satterlee," Peggy began, "was something taken from your drawer?"

"My wallet is missing from my purse, Peggy."

"I saw Alfred reach down and then slip something into his jacket," Peggy told her.

Mrs. Satterlee didn't answer right away. "You've risked a lot to tell me," she finally replied. "I'm sorry you've become part of this thing." She smiled at her two students. "I hope you both know how much I value your friendship."

"I couldn't let Alfred do that to you, Mrs. Satterlee," Peggy answered.

The phone rang. Mrs. Satterlee listened for a moment. "Don't leave," she whispered to Peggy. "A police officer is coming up."

Before she had finished on the phone, Mr. Lipman and an officer came into the room. The officer took

69

notes on Peggy's story and got all the details from Mrs. Satterlee. Then Mr. Lipman explained what had happened outside the classroom.

Alfred, when he was unexpectedly called to the office about class cuts, must have thrown away the evidence. Another student found the wallet in the trash can outside the attendance office and turned it in. That was why the office people knew the wallet had been stolen even before Mrs. Satterlee had discovered her loss.

Mr. Lipman held out the wallet. "The cards are here," he said, "but there's no money in it. How much did you have, Mrs. Satterlee?"

"Forty dollars," she answered. "I was going to buy food on the way home."

"Well, the next step is to find Alfred," Mr. Lipman said to the officer. "It's lunchtime now, which means he's probably off campus. We'll be waiting to greet him fifth period."

"By the way," Ron spoke up. "I think you should also know something else." He told the officer the whole story of what he and Peggy had heard near The Hamburger Hut.

"The people's description does fit Walter and Alfred," Mr. Lipman said.

"Yep," the officer agreed. "We have that case on our desk, too. Today looks like a two-for-one bargain." He made some notes in his book. "Thanks, kids. You've been a big help."

"I'm afraid there is going to be more for you, Peggy," Mr. Lipman said. "I'm sorry to have to tell you."

70

"More? I've told you all I know."

"I know that," Mr. Lipman said. "But you may have to tell it again. In court."

"It looks as if Alfred has broken parole on at least two counts," the officer said. "That means big trouble for him now. And . . ."

"And you're the eyewitness, Peggy," Mr. Lipman added.

Peggy and Ron stared at each other. "Whew," Ron said.

"Yecch," Peggy answered.

14

SUDDENLY EVERYTHING WAS DIFFERENT FOR Peggy and Ron. They opened the classroom door just a crack. It was important to know if anyone had seen them in a room with a police officer. To their relief, the hall was empty.

"Isn't that something?" Ron said. "Peggy Marklee, a prime witness in a court case."

"If I'm shaking like this now," Peggy answered, "I don't see how I'll ever speak in court."

"Let's not think about it anymore till later," Ron said. "Do you want some lunch?"

"I'm not hungry," Peggy answered.

"Some milk and a sandwich, maybe?"

"Well, maybe."

"We can get that in the fast line in the cafeteria," Ron said. "Let's go."

They hurried across the campus. Every time they passed a small group of people, Peggy wondered if they were talking about her. Even people she didn't know. It was an awful feeling.

"I don't think we should talk about this with other kids," Ron said as they entered the cafeteria.

"Don't worry," Peggy replied. "The only Jeff people I ever talk to are you and Roxanne and Cheryl. They'll hear it anyway. They hear everything."

Ron elbowed his way into the cafeteria crowd, pulling Peggy through, too.

"Let's talk about something else," she said.

"Like driver's licenses. I'm going to drive my mother all over the county this afternoon."

"Doesn't she drive?" Peggy asked.

"Oh sure," Ron answered. "But I can only drive with an adult along. So she puts up with me."

Peggy smiled at this picture of his mother.

Lunch period was almost over, when Ron and Peggy finally sat down with their food. Keeping an eye on the clock, they ate in silence. When they had almost finished, Peggy saw two girls looking at her.

"Those girls are talking about me," she whispered to Ron.

"How can you tell?"

"I saw one point toward me. The other had a sneer on her face. Watch. Now they're coming toward us." Peggy slid closer to Ron. "I'm in trouble," she whispered. "Look at their faces!"

The girls were moving slowly across the cafeteria. Ron reached for Peggy's hand under the table as they came nearer. "Hang on," he said softly out of the corner of his mouth.

"There she is!" one girl said as she passed behind Ron and Peggy. "That's the one who told the police. There's your little snitch."

"She'll wish she hadn't," the other added.

"Whew!" Ron said when the girls were gone. "It

looks as if Alfred's got himself a couple of tough white bodyguards."

"Those girls are mean," Peggy told him.

"They wouldn't dare try anything around school," Ron replied.

"No, but I don't spend twenty-four hours a day in school." Peggy became silent. She didn't want to talk about it. Already she was too scared to think.

"Now I wish I hadn't arranged to drive my mother on all her errands after school today," Ron said. "I should see you home instead."

"No! Don't change any plans that will help get your license," Peggy told Ron firmly. "I'll be okay." She wasn't sure it was true, but she wanted to believe it.

"I'll phone you tonight, then," Ron said. "Be careful. All afternoon."

Peggy was careful. Very careful. She didn't go near a rest room. She didn't go near her locker. She stayed in the main halls. But, somehow, she had the feeling that wherever she went she was being watched.

The afternoon seemed endless. When school was over, Peggy headed straight for home.

Before she had walked a full block, Peggy knew she was being followed. She could sense it. She didn't want to look back very often. That would make her look scared. All she could do was hurry home.

Breathing heavily and with her heart pounding, Peggy reached her front door. Quickly she unlocked it and stepped inside.

Each afternoon, her mother picked up transcripts from the court reporters. Peggy knew she would be alone for at least another hour. With the door safely locked behind her, she stood near the window, watching everyone who passed the house.

Peggy was beginning to wonder if it was all in her mind, when she spotted the two girls who had threatened her in the cafeteria. They were walking toward her house. Peggy jumped back out of sight. When they were in front of Peggy's window, they stopped. The girls looked the place over carefully. Then they moved on, glancing back as they left.

Peggy was in a panic. She tried to do her homework. Her pencil shook too much to write. She went to the kitchen to set the table for dinner. She dropped the first glass she picked up.

She turned on the radio and huddled in the big chair. She couldn't even keep her mind on the music. When the phone rang, Peggy's heart almost stopped.

She picked up the receiver as if it were wired to explode. She held the phone to her ear while she tried to find her voice. Peggy could hear breathing.

Then a husky female voice said, "You'll be sorry. If Alfred goes to jail, we'll take care of *you.*"

The phone clicked.

Peggy was left holding a dial tone.

15

THE NEXT PHONE CALL CAME SEVERAL HOURS later. It was Ron. Peggy told him about the girls who followed her home. This worried him. Then she told him about the phone call. He went up in smoke.

Peggy had never even heard some of the names he called the girls. She held the phone close to her ear, enjoying his anger.

"Listen," Ron ordered, "don't you set foot outside the door tomorrow till I'm with you."

"Don't worry!" Peggy hung up, smiling. Scared as she was, she loved it when Ron wanted to protect her.

Ron arrived the next morning, looking serious. "Did you tell your mom?" he asked as they walked.

"Sort of," Peggy answered. "I told her about the part with Mrs. Satterlee. But I didn't want to worry her about the threats."

"Peg, even if you didn't tell your mom everything, I think you definitely should tell Mr. Lipman about the threats. There should be some protection for you if you are expected to be a witness."

"I'd feel stupid going in and telling him I want protection."

"Even so, I think the school should know."

"Maybe." Peggy wanted to leave it at that. The idea of anyone seeing her go into Mr. Lipman's office seemed more dangerous than the threats.

"Be careful until I see you again fourth period," Ron told Peggy as they reached the school.

"I will, Ron. Thanks." Peggy started toward her class.

"Oh, Peggy!" She turned. Mr. Lipman was calling from his office door. "Come in for a minute, will you?"

Peggy ducked into the office. A policeman was sitting there, holding a paper.

"I'm really sorry to have to involve you, Peggy," Mr. Lipman said, "but Officer Lanahan has a subpoena to deliver to you."

"A what?" Peggy, feeling dizzy, touched the desk to steady herself.

"An order to appear in court," the officer explained. "The Alfred Curtis case," he added as if Peggy didn't know.

"They need you and Mrs. Satterlee," Mr. Lipman said, "and they've subpoenaed me, too. The hearing is scheduled for Thursday at ten at the juvenile court. We can go down in my car."

Peggy stood there, frozen. "What will I say?" she finally asked.

"Simply answer the questions."

"What if I'm too scared to talk?"

"Then whisper," Mr. Lipman said. His manner was kind. "Lots of people do."

Officer Lanahan rose to leave. "Sorry to involve you, Peggy. But you'll do fine."

Peggy gave him a faint smile.

"By the way," Mr. Lipman said as the officer closed the door, "I'm getting word that you're being threatened. Is that right?"

"Yes."

"Can you describe the girls?"

Peggy told him about the two girls who had made remarks in the cafeteria and had followed her home.

"I know who they are," Mr. Lipman said. "They're Toni and Jana. They like to play their tough act. But they're backing a bad-news kid here. Alfred is going to lead them into big trouble."

"Mr. Lipman," the secretary broke in, "you have some parents waiting."

"Be right there." He turned to Peggy. "I'll see that you aren't troubled by those girls."

Peggy turned to smile. Mr. Lipman tossed her a friendly wave as she left the office.

It was almost time for the late bell. Peggy hurried to her locker. As she was opening it, a girl came up behind her and said, "Toni and Jana sent you a message." Handing Peggy a folded paper, the girl took off.

Peggy held the note as if it were a bomb. With shaking hands, she unfolded the paper and read the message: "IF ALFRED GOES TO JAIL, YOU'LL BE SORRY!"

Peggy shivered. She shoved the note into her purse and went to class.

The words in the note burned in Peggy's mind all morning. When she could finally whisper the whole story to Ron, before fourth period, Peggy started to feel better.

Then Roxanne and Cheryl arrived.

"Well," Cheryl said as she dropped her books on the desk. "We heard all about it."

"Did you hear that I have to appear in court, too?" Peggy asked.

"Yep," said Roxanne. "And that you've been getting threats from Jana and Toni."

"You're right, Peg," Ron said, laughing. "They do hear everything."

"Okay," Peggy said, testing Roxanne and Cheryl. "When is the court hearing?"

"Thursday at ten," they answered together.

Peggy threw up her hands and turned to Ron. "With these two around, who needs a newspaper?"

Roxanne shot a look toward the two empty seats in the back. "It's nice without them, isn't it? They locked Alfred up yesterday for breaking parole. And I heard that Walter is being held for questioning."

"But Jana and Toni are loose," Cheryl said. "They are the real danger right now."

"You two had better stick with us at lunchtime," Roxanne said. "You're both so new to the school, it'll be good for Jana and Toni to see you with us old-timers. We went to grammar school with those two. We know how they operate."

"Do we ever!" Cheryl chimed in. "They were trouble, even in the fourth grade."

Peggy looked at Ron. He seemed agreeable to the plan.

"And I'll see you to and from school," Ron whispered.

"With all of us working at it, you'll get through Thursday somehow," Roxanne said.

Peggy smiled an uncertain thank-you to all of them.

16

ON THURSDAY MORNING, PEGGY AWOKE WITH A lump in her throat. How will I ever make it through a court hearing? she wondered. I wish Ron could come along. What will I do when Alfred looks at me? And his attorney questions me? And the judge stares at me? She pulled the blankets over her head and hoped it would all go away. Her seven o'clock alarm brought her back to the real world.

Three hours until ten o'clock, Peggy thought. Will I live that long?

At nine thirty Peggy and Mrs. Satterlee trailed Mr. Lipman out to the school parking lot. Now ten o'clock is coming much too soon, Peggy decided.

A half hour later, they walked into the waiting room of the juvenile court. Mr. Lipman spoke to a woman at a desk. Then he told Peggy and Mrs. Satterlee they would have to wait for the district attorney to meet with them.

As Peggy sat on the bench studying the people, she felt sorry for the mothers. Some of them were trying to keep restless babies happy while they waited.

"There's Alfred's mother," Mr. Lipman whispered.

"She looks nice," Peggy replied softly.

"And Alfred's been nothing but trouble to her for years," Mr. Lipman added.

"Where's Alfred?" Peggy asked.

"He's in back, probably. There's a room with a TV where the kids wait for their hearing."

"I'll die when Alfred looks at me."

Mr. Lipman gave Peggy a reassuring smile. "You'll be fine."

If only Ron were here, Peggy kept thinking. Things are better when he's around. Her mind wandered off.

"Will you step in here now?" an attendant said. "Your case will be coming up next."

In a small office, the district attorney studied a folder. He questioned the three of them.

"I think the case is ready to go," he said. "Just wait here until you're called, please."

"The Curtis case is next," a voice in the lobby announced.

They came for Mr. Lipman. Peggy and Mrs. Satterlee waited nervously while he was gone. Then Mrs. Satterlee was called. Peggy, alone in the room, cleared her throat over and over. She was too hot. She was too cold. She was going to be sick.

Peggy finally heard her name called. "Peggy Marklee, please."

It was unreal. Peggy Marklee must be someone else. Not the girl walking into the courtroom.

Peggy was led to the witness stand. "Raise your

right hand. Do you swear to tell the truth . . ." Peggy heard herself saying, "I do." The voice seemed shaky and weak. She kept her eyes on the floor.

"Peggy," the lawyer began, "will you look around this room and tell me if you see Alfred Curtis?"

Peggy raised her eyes and nodded toward Alfred. "That's him." Alfred showed no sign of life.

"Now, Peggy, tell us what you saw in fourth period on October 29."

Peggy told exactly what she had seen at Mrs. Satterlee's desk.

"You saw Alfred take a paper clip from the teacher's desk? And then you saw him reach down to a lower drawer, take something, and slip it inside his jacket?"

"Yes, that's right," Peggy agreed.

"How close to the desk were you?"

"About from here to that table."

"Show us how Alfred slipped the object into his jacket."

Peggy looked confused.

"Just stand up and show us the motions he went through."

Peggy stood up and slipped a hand inside the opening of her sweater.

"Since this took place in the front of the room, why didn't the whole class see it?"

"I guess everyone else was turned toward Walter. He was having a coughing spell."

"Why were you watching Alfred instead?"

"Because I knew. I had it figured out. When Walter started some kind of action, Alfred was always up to something." Peggy's knees were shaking, but she had found her voice.

Alfred and his lawyer whispered to each other. The lawyer shook his head. Alfred's face was like a mask.

"Any further questions?" the judge asked.

"No further questions, Your Honor."

"Thank you, Peggy. That's all."

She was led out of the courtroom.

Mr. Lipman and Mrs. Satterlee were waiting for her. Peggy suddenly felt strong. "I did it," she crowed. "I spoke up. I got the story all straight. And they could hear me."

"It's not fun to testify against someone," Mrs. Satterlee said.

"But Alfred seemed to know he couldn't fight this one," Mr. Lipman said. "Come on, let's get out of here. Alfred's parole officer will phone me after the verdict is reached."

Peggy rode in silence. She had done well. But, instead of feeling proud, she felt awful. Alfred was sure to go to jail. He had broken parole. All the way back that message kept running through Peggy's mind. *If Alfred goes to jail, you'll be sorry. If Alfred goes to jail . . .*

"I'll drop you at your house, Peggy," Mr. Lipman said as they neared the school. "There's no point in your being anywhere near Toni and Jana today. Feelings will be running high."

"Will it be any better tomorrow if Alfred goes to jail?" Peggy asked.

"Toni and Jana are hotheaded," Mr. Lipman said.

"But they'll find a new hero as soon as Alfred is out of reach. They always seem to back people who are on their way to jail." He smiled at Peggy. "But we can handle it."

When the car stopped in front of Peggy's house, Mrs. Satterlee turned to her. "I hope you know how grateful I am to you for coming to my aid, Peggy. You were an unwilling witness, but a very fine one."

"You're a good teacher, Mrs. Satterlee. There's no way I could have let Alfred do that to you." With a wave Peggy hurried inside.

The long afternoon was broken only by a call from Ron. Peggy told him all about the court hearing. Then she said, "We'll just have to wait to hear the verdict. Maybe I have a problem, and maybe I don't."

17

THE NEXT MORNING, WHEN RON AND PEGGY PASSED Mr. Lipman's office, he asked them to come in. "They're sending Alfred to one of the Youth Authority detention centers," he told them. "So that means Toni and Jana may go off the deep end today. Don't leave campus. Eat in the cafeteria and stay with friends. Who are your friends, by the way, Peggy?"

"Roxanne Milton and Cheryl King."

"I'll talk with them," Mr. Lipman said. "Stay with them at lunchtime. Their crowd will be able to handle anything that might come up."

"I usually eat with Ron," Peggy told him.

"Let's keep this strictly among girls," Mr. Lipman answered. "I'm sure Ron wants to be nearby, but let's keep the boys out of it."

Peggy nodded her acceptance of the plan. Then she turned to leave with Ron. She raised a questioning eyebrow at him.

"It'll be okay," he whispered.

Peggy didn't talk to anyone until fourth period. She could hardly wait to see Roxanne and Cheryl. They'd be dying to learn all about the court hearing.

Instead of their usual bubbling entrance, Roxanne and Cheryl were whispering behind their hands as they came in. They hardly noticed Peggy. During class they kept passing notes and exchanging glances. Peggy felt completely cut off.

When the lunch bell rang, Roxanne finally spoke to Peggy. "Girl, you stay right with us. Hear?"

When Roxanne used that tone, Peggy didn't ask questions. She signaled good-by to Ron and waited for orders.

Cheryl motioned for her to come along. With Peggy between them, Roxanne and Cheryl moved down the hall toward the cafeteria.

Outside the cafeteria a small crowd had gathered. Toni and Jana were in the middle.

"There's the little snitch. She's the one who sent Alfred to jail," one girl jeered.

Roxanne and Cheryl kept their eyes forward. With Peggy between them, they walked into the cafeteria and joined the line. Mr. Lipman was standing near the food service.

With their trays filled, the three girls moved out into the table area. No one spoke. It all fell into place without words. Roxanne motioned for Peggy to sit down. Within seconds, Peggy was surrounded by twenty-five black girls. They calmly set their trays down as if they always surrounded a white girl when they ate. Nothing in their manner showed they might be expecting trouble.

But trouble was coming.

Toni and Jana were moving across the cafeteria. In a moment they stood right behind Roxanne and Cheryl and Peggy. They had on their toughest looks.

"You would think those girls would stand behind their black brother, wouldn't you?" Toni said loudly to Jana.

"We have to do it for them," Jana answered in a taunting tone. "Isn't that something?"

Roxanne looked up calmly. "Alfred would be a hood in any color," she said with dignity. "But I guess some people like hoods."

"Can you believe these two girls?" Toni went on. "For a friend they pick a person who sent a man to jail."

"Alfred sent himself to jail," Cheryl replied. Like Roxanne, she was all courtesy. "And now, if you'll excuse us, we'd like to finish our lunch."

"Listen," Jana growled, coming closer. Her fists were tightening up. Her eyes were flashing. "We came here to settle a debt. Not to be put off."

Jana grabbed a piece of pie from one of the trays. Toni snatched a bowl of chili. They raised their arms, ready to throw the food.

Instantly, Roxanne and Cheryl were on their feet, facing Jana and Toni.

"Go ahead. Throw it," Roxanne said. "Feel free to look stupid! But don't expect anyone from this group to join you in a food fight." Roxanne looked around at the twenty-five girls. Their eyes were on her, waiting for some signal. "These ladies have entirely too much class to throw food."

Jana and Toni still held the food in the air. Their eyes searched the cafeteria. They seemed to be looking for someone. When they looked toward the doorway, suddenly everything changed.

A tall young man with tattooed arms and a leather vest stepped inside the door. Jana poked Toni with her elbow. "Look, Jake's here now," she whispered.

Making a big thing of it, Toni and Jana set the food on a nearby table. With disdain they turned away from Roxanne's crowd.

"Sorry. We've got more important business than this right now," Jana said over her shoulder. "There's someone we have to see."

"Don't let us keep you," Roxanne called after her.

Jana and Toni sailed over to Jake. Squealing with phony delight, they fell into his arms. They knew all eyes were on them, and they played their scene to the fullest.

Anyone could see that they had carefully planned Jake's entrance. He was supposed to show up looking like the big gorilla—the head of their goon squad.

But the plan had not worked. Roxanne wouldn't go for the free-for-all. So now they had to use Jake to escape.

Jake, with a girl in each arm, moved toward the door. "Ooo eee . . . wait till you two see what I have in the parking lot," he said loudly to Toni and Jana and the whole cafeteria. "Talk about wheels!"

As the trio disappeared from sight, a murmur spread through the crowd. Roxanne's twenty-five girls grinned.

Peggy took her first deep breath and let out a sigh. "Hey, thanks, everybody," she said to the crowd. Leaning over to Roxanne and Cheryl, she whispered, "You two are really something."

89

The whole place began to buzz. Everyone had to compare notes.

"You were so good!" Peggy told Roxanne. "As if you had been rehearsing the scene for weeks."

"Not weeks—years," Roxanne corrected. "We've been waiting for a chance to put those two down since they stole the fourth-grade book club money. They told the teacher they had seen us take it."

"I'd say the score is even now," Peggy told Roxanne. "More than even. You're way ahead."

Roxanne and Cheryl were beaming with delight. Peggy felt excited to have been a part of their private drama.

Then, for the first time, Peggy realized that Ron had been watching everything from the doorway. When she caught his eye, he grinned and gestured with his hands that it was all over. Things were okay. Better than okay.

The crowd began to break up. Peggy took her tray to the window and went over to Ron.

"That was beautiful," he whispered. His mouth was so close to her ear, it almost seemed like a kiss. Peggy shivered; her cheeks flushed. "I was really proud of you," he added.

"I was scared," Peggy confessed.

"Me too," Ron confided. "Who knows what it might have turned into."

"Weren't Roxanne and Cheryl fantastic?" Peggy raved. "And their whole crowd!"

"Really classy," Ron agreed.

18

PEGGY AND RON WALKED SLOWLY TOWARD THE center of campus. They knew the fifth-period bell would ring any minute, but they really didn't care. A tardy bell seemed like nothing after what they'd just been through.

"Hey, you two," someone called across the courtyard. Still tense, Peggy and Ron whirled around to face the caller. It was Roxanne, trying to catch their attention as she and Cheryl hurried toward them.

Roxanne was still glowing with excitement. Her victory showed in the way she walked.

"We've just decided to throw a winners party tonight," she told them. "Will you come?"

Peggy and Ron looked at each other and then nodded eagerly.

"Cheryl's folks both work this evening, so we're going to cook dinner at her house. We're inviting a couple of guys we know from church—and you two. After Alfred, you should get to know some real black men. Darrell and Michael are college freshmen instead of hoods."

"Sounds great," Ron answered.

"Sure does!" Peggy agreed.

"Cheryl's a real cook," Roxanne explained. "She learned French Creole cooking from her grandmother in New Orleans."

"Mmm. Wouldn't want to miss that!" Peggy and Ron responded together.

"Here, I'll draw you a map," Cheryl said. "My place is within walking distance of school, but Cadiz Court is tricky to find."

They all sat down on a nearby wall while Cheryl worked out the directions. "There you are," she said at last. "Can you figure out my scribbles?"

Ron and Peggy looked.

"Sure."

"Easy."

"How does six o'clock sound?" Roxanne looked around for approval. "Okay with everyone?"

"Great."

"Can we bring something?" Peggy asked.

"No. Just come."

Roxanne and Cheryl started buzzing with plans. "Let's cut afternoon classes and go home for some money and then go to the market," Cheryl said.

Roxanne and Cheryl began making a shopping list. With a wave, Ron and Peggy left them.

"We're late for class," Ron pointed out.

"I know," Peggy replied. "I was just thinking how awful it will be to walk in and have everyone stare. Especially today, after that big scene in the cafeteria."

"So, let's cut fifth and sixth," Ron suggested.

Peggy stopped walking and stared at him. Ron

looked at her. "Sound too wild? Two whole hours of not being where you're supposed to be?" There was a twinkle in his eyes, a tease in his manner.

"Yeah," Peggy said very slowly. "It really is wild. I never cut a class in my life."

"Except for that first day at Jeff," Ron said.

"But I wasn't even enrolled in any classes yet. And, besides, I was inside the school. What do people do when they cut?"

Ron was amused. "They go to the library and read a book. Or they steal a car and head for the lake. Or they go under the bleachers and get stoned. Or . . ."

Peggy began to laugh at Ron's teasing. "This time count me in," she said. "What shall we do with our two hours?"

Ron could hardly believe his ears. He was expecting her to decide cutting was wrong. Quickly, he began to think. "How much time do you need to dress for the party?"

"Maybe an hour."

"If we get you home by four, that's plenty of time, isn't it?"

"Sure."

"So we have quite a bit of free time. Any ideas?"

"I just don't want to be seen by all the other kids this afternoon," Peggy answered. "They probably think I looked like a dummy in the cafeteria."

"You and your dummy thing. Forget it!"

Peggy glanced at Ron, feeling embarrassed, but pleased by his confidence in her.

"Why don't we go down to the shopping mall and get lost in the crowd," Ron suggested. "Hold it. First, let's see if we have enough for bus fare." He started counting his loose change.

Peggy emptied her coin purse into his hand. "We're okay," she told him. "I have a five-dollar bill put away, too."

Ron looked at his watch. "The bus comes at twenty after."

"I want to phone Mom first and tell her where I'll be," Peggy said.

"You *what?*" Ron almost shouted. "You want to tell your mother you're cutting?"

"Sure. She knew today would be different. I kind of told her about Toni and Jana. So I'll just tell her it all came out fine and we're celebrating."

"And that the celebration will continue at Cheryl's this evening, too," Ron added as a joke. "Might as well clear it all at one time."

"Might as well," Peggy repeated. "Good idea."

Ron listened in disbelief as Peggy asked permission from her mother to cut school.

Peggy hung up the phone, looking satisfied. "Mom says she's relieved that things worked out, and that some celebration seems in order. And thanks for letting her know what we're doing."

"Fantastic lady," Ron murmured.

As they started across the campus toward the bus stop, Peggy discovered how many people were not in their classes. "I had no idea!" she exclaimed.

They passed two girls writing a paper together. Peggy knew they were in her second-period class. She gave them a shy smile.

"We saw you in the cafeteria," one of them said. "That was marvelous."

"I would have been scared to death," the other girl added.

"I was!" Peggy told them.

"What's your name, by the way?" one of the girls called. "We're Elaine and Rita."

"I'm Peggy. And this is Ron."

"We've seen you sitting alone in class, Peggy. Why don't you sit with us?"

"I will—tomorrow. Thanks," Peggy replied.

"You've got it made," Ron chanted as they moved on. "Miss New Girl is in."

A boy was coming toward them. "You were great at lunch today!" he said as he passed.

"Thanks," Peggy answered, surprised.

"Who was that?" Ron asked.

"Some guy in my first-period class," she said with a shrug.

"You've come out of the shadows. They all know you now. I'm walking with a celebrity."

Peggy sensed that Ron wasn't entirely happy about her sudden fame.

"I'm not really the celebrity type," she told him. "Just a few friends will do."

Ron answered with a grateful smile. "Then count me in."

"Don't worry," Peggy answered. "You're already counted."

19

IT WAS A TEN-MINUTE BUS RIDE TO THE WOODMONT Shopping Mall. To Peggy's amazement, the route was sprinkled all the way with high school students.

"Who's still in classes?" she asked Ron. "Is it always like this?"

"Worse on Fridays," Ron told her. He grinned at her. "Learning some new things about public school, huh?" He pointed an accusing finger at Peggy. "And you're guilty . . . guilty . . . guilty, Peggy Marklee . . . guilty just like the rest."

"Even guiltier," she answered with a smug little smile, "because I'm enjoying it so much."

Ron smiled back. "How about that!"

The bus pulled up to the shopping center and Peggy and Ron got off. As they stepped into the music-filled mall, the world slowed down. Everything seemed to move at a gentler pace. The temperature was just right. The lighting was soft. Planter boxes filled with trees and blooming plants lined the walkways. Fountains sparkled and danced. The mall was made for strolling.

Ron reached for Peggy's hand, and they walked along, looking at window displays.

"Anyplace in particular you want to go? Anything you want to look at?" Ron asked.

"Not really," Peggy answered. "It's fun just being with you."

Ron squeezed her hand. They kept walking.

The window displays were lavish but could have been empty and Peggy still would have felt alive and excited.

Peggy and Ron just strolled and listened to the music. After a while they came to a wide area in the mall. Sunlight filtered through the skylight.

Peggy tugged on Ron's arm. "Look at those chrysanthemums."

As they stood there admiring the mass of gold, a little girl toddled up to the flowers in front of Peggy and started to smell them.

"Look at that," Ron commented. "So tiny. She hardly has to stoop over to be on eye level with a flower."

The child lifted her eyes and solemnly studied Ron and Peggy.

"A little Asian doll," Peggy whispered to Ron, "with those dark eyes and that shiny black hair."

Peggy smiled, but the child remained serious.

"What's your name?" Peggy asked, stooping down to the child's level.

No answer.

"Where's your mother?" Ron tried.

"No answer.

They looked around the mall. Someone must surely be watching the child. No one seemed to be, though.

"Is your daddy here?" Peggy asked her. "Your big sister . . . Mommy?" She was trying them all, hoping one of the words would give some clue.

Suddenly the little girl began to tell them all about it. She chattered and bubbled.

"I can't understand a thing she's telling me," Peggy whispered.

"I can't even tell what language she's speaking," Ron replied. His eyes searched the mall. "There's got to be somebody nearby looking for her."

"Let's go look for your mommy," Peggy suggested to the child. She held out her hand. The little girl took it, trustingly. "I wonder what the word 'mommy' is in her language," Peggy said to Ron. He shook his head.

The three of them started walking in a big circle around the mall, expecting someone to run up and claim the child. The little girl reached her other hand out to Ron. Smiling down at her, he took it.

"Let's check with that security guard," Ron suggested. He was pointing to a man with a walkie-talkie.

"Have you had any lost-child calls?" Ron asked the guard.

"No, but I'll check on it," the man replied. He patted the little head as he called. "No report," he finally said, "but there's bound to be one soon. Why don't you just sit down on that bench with her till we hear something?"

Peggy and Ron led their little friend to a bench. Seated between them, she soon discovered the zipper on Peggy's purse. While she was happily occupied, Peggy and Ron scanned the crowd, looking for a worried parent.

The smell of fresh-baked cookies drifted across from The Cookie House.

"Just a moment, little one," Peggy told the child. "I need to get into my purse." Taking the handbag, she removed her wallet and then handed the bag back to the child.

"Will you stay with her, Ron, while I go across the way?" Peggy asked.

"Sure."

Peggy followed the delicious fragrance straight to the display cases in The Cookie House. "I'll take one frosted gingerbread boy," she told the clerk, "and a dozen lemon chip cookies."

Returning to the bench, Peggy handed the gingerbread boy to the child.

As the little girl nibbled, the cookie fast became a frosting-smeared mess. And so did the child's face.

"Oh, I almost forgot. Here." Peggy handed the cookie bag to Ron. "These are for the big child."

"I'm not lost," he said.

"That's why you only got lemon chip instead of gingerbread boys," Peggy told him.

Ron reached over with his fist, as if to punch her knee. Instead, the fist came down gently as a pat. Peggy melted inside.

Where *is* this child's mother? Peggy wondered. Our afternoon is going to be gone very soon.

Within seconds a different security officer was coming down the mall with a distraught woman at his side. The frail-looking little mother, carrying a baby, was sobbing. The officer was trying in vain to reassure her.

"Look," Peggy said to the child, "is that your mommy?" The little girl waved the remains of the cookie, smiling for the first time.

The mother rushed over, crying and talking and hugging and scolding. The little girl took it all calmly.

"I think it's the mother who needed the ginger-bread boy," Peggy whispered.

"Wonder how lemon chip would work," Ron mused.

Not being able to converse with the woman, the officer finally laid a comforting hand on her shoulder and waved good-by. Only after he left did the woman begin to relax a little.

Ron opened the cookie bag and held it out to her.

"I don't yet speak English," she said haltingly.

"Have a cookie." Ron handed her one from the bag. Then he and Peggy each took one and started eating.

The woman pointed to the remains of the child's gingerbread cookie. "Thank you," she said shyly.

The little girl began to chatter to her mother, who put an arm around the child. Then the child started chattering to Ron and Peggy.

The child and her mother stood up to leave. "Thank you," the mother said to Peggy with great courtesy. "Thank you," she said, turning to Ron. "Thank you," she said, finally, to both of them.

100

Ron and Peggy smiled at the woman. They waved to their little friend, until finally she had disappeared down the mall.

"Imagine losing your child someplace where you can't speak the language," Peggy said.

"There was real terror in that mother's eyes," Ron replied.

"Well, I know how it is to be surrounded by strangers," Peggy said. "But strangers who speak another language—that's something else."

Ron nodded. "Do you think we'd better be getting home?"

"I've lost track of time," Peggy answered. "What time is it?" She leaned over and held Ron's wrist to look at his watch. Her head was very close to his face. Ron brushed her hair with a kiss.

"You're nice, Peg," he said softly. "I like the way you treated that child and her mother."

Peggy shivered. They stood up to leave. Ron took her hand.

As they passed The Cookie House, Peggy paused, tugging Ron to a stop.

"What do you think? Should we take some gingerbread people to Roxanne and Cheryl tonight?"

"Good idea," Ron agreed. "Gingerbread cookies seem to speak some universal language. I guess they can say 'That was a great victory.'"

After ordering an assortment of fancy-frosted cookies, packed in a gift box, they went on toward the bus stop.

"We didn't have much chance to talk," Ron said.

"I'm glad we'll be together again this evening. Otherwise I would feel cheated."

"I'm glad, too," Peggy told him. "I'll go home and try to look gorgeous for you."

"You don't have to," Ron replied. "But I'll enjoy it." There was a twinkle in his eyes. "And I'll see what I can do about myself for you, too."

They were nearing the bus stop.

"I'll come by at five thirty," Ron said.

"Fine."

"Wish I could pick you up in a car."

"Someday," Peggy said with a smile.

Their separate buses arrived. They parted with a wave.

20

Peggy dreamily ignored the blur of passing scenes as the bus moved along. So many things had happened so fast—she had to have time to think.

One by one, she reviewed each event of the day. The tension of the morning. Knowing Toni and Jana were out to get her. The fear that Roxanne and Cheryl were not pleased with her. The angry confrontation in the cafeteria. The surprise ending. Ron being gentle with a child. Just being with Ron. Being with Ron. Being with Ron. She didn't want to let go of that one, even to dream about the evening ahead.

Peggy put her key in the lock of her front door. Somehow she knew that her mother would be waiting. It suddenly dawned on Peggy that there was nothing reasonable at all about her earlier phone call to her mother. What was I thinking of? Here I've only been out with a boy once in my life, for one hour, and I phone home and say, "Mom, I'm cutting my afternoon classes and going off with this boy."

Did I really hear her answer? Or did I just hear what I wanted to hear? I'll bet she's plenty upset!

Peggy tiptoed past the doorway of the den.

"Hello," her mother called.

Peggy couldn't tell anything from her mother's greeting.

"Hi," she answered. Too embarrassed to stick around, Peggy slipped into her room, gathered up a few things, and locked herself in the bathroom.

As the hot water poured down on her, she tried to think of different ways to explain everything. But how? How can it be done? In only a few minutes, how could her mother possibly catch up on a court hearing, threats of personal injury, new friends who protected her, cutting school, an invitation to a victory celebration?

"And a boy who likes me!" Peggy shouted that one out loud to the shower. "Hear that? A boy who likes me!"

A knock on the bathroom door brought Peggy back to her problem.

"Are you all right? I heard you calling, but I couldn't understand what you said."

Peggy stuck her head out of the shower. "I'm fine." Then she retreated again into the hot stream.

I'm going to have to talk about it with her, Peggy decided. Somehow, she's got to understand. I can't be this happy all alone.

Peggy relaxed under the hot water. What's Ron going to say to his mother? she wondered. Do you suppose he's in the shower, too? I wonder if that hair over his ears curls when it's wet. I wonder what he's going to wear. I wonder if he's wondering about me.

Dripping, Peggy stepped from the shower and groped for the towel. She splashed herself lavishly

104

with the cologne her St. Anne's friends had given her
and dusted herself with the matching bath powder.
Then, wrapped in her terry cloth robe, Peggy
headed for her room.

Mrs. Marklee was sitting on the bed, waiting. "I
think we need to talk, Peggy."

"I know. That was a weird phone call at noontime,
wasn't it?"

"Well, it's not just the phone call, Peggy. It's the
last few days. No . . . more than that. It's the last few
weeks. So much has been happening."

"I haven't done anything wrong," Peggy answered
quickly.

"That's not what I'm trying to say. It's just that so
many really big things have happened all at once."

Peggy opened her mouth, but her mother went
on.

"It's like wishing it would rain and suddenly you're
in a flood. Too much too quickly. Honey, I don't want
you to be swept away."

"You mean by Ron?" Peggy asked. "Listen, Mom,
do you know what we did when we cut school this
afternoon? We sat in the Woodmont Shopping Mall
and fed a gingerbread cookie to a little lost child.
Pretty wild, huh?"

Mrs. Marklee shook her head and smiled.

"And do you know how wild we're going to be
tonight? Two girl friends are cooking dinner for us.
And we're getting there by walking, because Ron
doesn't have a license yet."

"It's funny, Peggy, these are exactly the things you
wanted to happen when you changed to a big high

105

school," Mrs. Marklee said. "So why am I worrying?"

"Because mothers usually worry," Peggy told her. "But listen, Mom, let me tell you about what happened at noontime. This is really something."

Peggy flopped across the bed and started. In telling the incidents to her mother, she even discovered some details she had already forgotten. Together they shuddered and laughed their way through the story.

The report ended with Ron. "He's nice, Mom. Really nice."

The clock by her bed caught Peggy's eye. She jumped up. "Oh no! He'll be here soon. And I'm not ready." Peggy turned to her dressing. Her mother left her alone.

I hope he likes what I'm wearing, Peggy thought. She studied the total effect in the mirror. I do look better than I did this afternoon. But is my dress right? I think Cheryl and Roxanne will really dress up. That's my guess. But what if they don't? I might be dressed all wrong. Oh well, they'll be nice about it if I blow it.

By the time Ron knocked on the door, Peggy was a mass of doubts.

I just haven't done this enough to be very good at it, she thought as she hurried to the door. But, then, neither has he. So we'll be okay together. We'll be o-kay.

21

PEGGY STOOD AT THE DOOR. "BYE," SHE WHISPERED to her mother. For a moment Peggy hesitated, her hand on the knob. Then she took a deep breath and opened the door.

Peggy was stunned by the change in Ron. "Wow! You look gorgeous."

"Gorgeous!" Ron repeated after her. "That wasn't what I had in mind. I was thinking more in terms of . . ." He paused to clear his throat and flick a speck of lint from his jacket. "Shall we say 'mature good taste,' 'manly,' 'well-groomed'?"

"You're all of that," Peggy assured him, "but you're gorgeous, too." She ran her hand lightly down the lapel of his coat. "I love the shirt. And such a nice jacket."

Ron glowed. He had been studying Peggy. "Now, speaking of gorgeous," he said, "you are!"

"Oh, it's just a little something I . . ." Peggy broke up, laughing. "Let's face it. It's the only dress-up dress I have. I'm glad you like it."

"I do."

Peggy looked beyond Ron to the street. She was

surprised to see his parents' car there—with his mother in it.

"This form of transportation is called 'Mother Express,'" he explained. "I didn't want you to get all dressed up and then blow away in the wind."

"That was nice thinking," Peggy told him.

Ron took Peggy around to the driver's side and opened the door. She slid into the seat, greeting Mrs. Loftus.

"This car comes equipped with a mother," Mrs. Loftus told Peggy, "although Ron would prefer a model without one."

"Well, it certainly beats being windblown tonight," Peggy replied. "Thank you."

Peggy admired the way Ron handled the car. Just another month, she told herself. Just one month and he'll have a license to drive alone.

Ron pulled into Cadiz Court and scanned the apartment numbers.

"Will you want a ride home?" Mrs. Loftus asked as Ron stopped the car. "You could phone when you're ready to leave."

Ron looked at Peggy.

"Oh no, we can walk home," Peggy told her. "But thanks, anyway."

With a wave, Mrs. Loftus drove away, and Ron and Peggy walked up to Cheryl's doorway. Peggy felt nervous and excited. But she tried to look as if she had been going out with boys for years.

Ron ran his hand around his shirt collar. Then he tugged on his jacket sleeves.

"Nervous?" Peggy whispered.

"Nervous? Me? Why, I've been taking out pretty girls for . . ." Ron looked at Peggy and grinned. "For all of fifteen minutes," he finished.

They were laughing together when Roxanne opened the door.

"Come in," she said.

Peggy and Ron stood on the doorstep staring at her shimmering blue dress.

"Wow! You look like a model, Roxanne," Peggy said.

"Or, as Alfred and Walter would say, Ooo eee," Ron teased.

Roxanne was pleased. She pulled Ron and Peggy inside. In the kitchen Cheryl, with an apron over her party dress, greeted them warmly.

"It smells wonderful," Peggy told her. "Can I help?"

"No. It's all under control. But you can help eat it pretty soon."

Peggy set the box of cookies on the kitchen table.

"Just a little thanks for you two," she explained.

"Peggy, you don't have to thank us," Cheryl answered. "As a matter of fact, we should thank you. We've been waiting a long time to put Toni and Jana in their place."

"It's more than that," Peggy replied, suddenly feeling shy. "You're my first friends at Jeff."

Cheryl's answer was soft. "And we're the first black friends you've ever had. Right?" she asked.

"Something like that," Peggy agreed. Tears were so close that she didn't dare look into Cheryl's eyes.

"Come on!" Cheryl broke the tension. "Let's add

109

two more new friends to the list." She steered Peggy and Ron into the living room.

Roxanne introduced the young man standing near her. "This is Michael Brandon." She touched Michael's arm. "And that's Darrell Gilmore."

Ron shook hands with them and Peggy smiled. Darrell likes Cheryl's cooking, she thought. He looks well fed and happy. And Michael looks right for Roxanne. Tall . . . basketball star, I'll bet.

"Help yourselves to chips and dips," Cheryl told everyone.

When they sat down, Peggy was overcome by nervousness. What will we talk about? These are grown-up college men. To them, Ron and I are just a couple of kids. She took some chips to keep her hands busy.

Ron started the talk. "Are you by any chance a runner?" he asked Michael.

Michael looked surprised. "Does it show that much? My shapely legs or something?"

"You run out by the Point," Ron went on. "I've seen you go by my aunt's house."

"You're right. That's my route. I like to run where there's a view at least part of the way. The Point is one of my favorite spots."

"Mine too!" Peggy chimed in. The thought of the Point made her heart leap.

"Are you out for track?" Ron asked.

"In high school I was," Michael said. "Now I just run to get the cobwebs out of my brain after studying."

Peggy saw how easily conversations can take off.

She jumped in. "What are you two studying?"

"Recreation education," Michael told her. "Work with kids . . . senior citizens . . . sports."

"Like a community center director?" Ron asked.

"Exactly," Michael answered.

"And you, Darrell?" Ron inquired.

"I'm going into accounting."

Peggy was proud. She had no idea Ron could handle social situations so easily. With him taking the lead, she even felt that she could talk, too.

"By the way," Darrell said, "we were told this is a victory celebration tonight. What are we celebrating?"

"Oh, that's a story," Ron said with a gleam in his eyes. "That *is* a story."

And then it was all spilling out. Walter and Alfred . . . the orange cap . . . Walter's attention-getting tactics . . . the missing vocabulary answer key . . . the gold pen . . . the mugging at The Hamburger Hut . . . the stolen wallet . . . the court hearing.

With Cheryl calling in comments from the kitchen, and Roxanne and Peggy decorating the story as Ron told it, Darrell and Michael began to feel the drama of the situation.

Peggy simply had to take over the cafeteria scene. She couldn't let anyone else tell how Roxanne and Cheryl stood up to Toni and Jana, and how all the girls kept calm while Toni and Jana were grabbing the food. When she got to the part where Toni and Jana had to use Jake as an excuse to get out of their own mess, everyone was cheering and clapping.

111

"That was worth waiting six years to see," Roxanne told them. "It was beautiful."

"And now everyone in the school knows who Peggy is," Cheryl called in from the kitchen. "She's a celebrity."

Peggy was embarrassed. "I'm not the type," she said softly, almost to herself. "I just want a few friends." She ducked her head. "Like now," she added, glancing up shyly.

Ron flashed Peggy a special smile. She lowered her eyes.

"And now, let's celebrate," Cheryl said. She had taken off her apron and was motioning for them to come to the candlelit table.

"This time you have outdone your grandmother," Darrell told Cheryl as he eyed the spread.

"No one outdoes Grandma!" Cheryl told him. "That's why she's been cooking for one of New Orleans' fanciest restaurants for thirty-five years."

"Being second to Cheryl's grandmother is still being way ahead," Roxanne pointed out.

"I certainly agree," Ron added. "I've never seen anything like this."

They all relaxed, talking mostly about things Roxanne and Cheryl had done with Michael and Darrell. Ron and Peggy listened a lot, but they never felt left out.

After the last bite of pecan pie disappeared, Cheryl suggested, "Why don't you move to the living room and get comfortable? I'll bring some espresso."

Cheryl served the very strong coffee in tiny cups. Peggy found herself enjoying the new taste.

Roxanne set the box of gingerbread cookies on the coffee table. "Look at these beautiful cookies Peggy brought," she said.

As she shifted the cookies around to show off the different designs, everyone raved.

"Someday I'm going to try making things like that," Cheryl told them all. "I've thought of becoming a fancy baker for a pastry shop."

"You should, Cheryl," Ron agreed. "Believe me, you really should. Your customers would love anything you made."

The conversation was easy. When Ron finally looked at his watch, he was surprised.

"This is too pleasant for us to break it up," he said, "but I'm afraid we'll have to leave."

Michael and Darrell said they needed to get home, too.

"It was a perfect victory celebration," Peggy told the girls. "Fantastic, in fact."

"Want to go another round with Toni and Jana so we can celebrate again?" Cheryl asked with a sly grin.

"How about just the celebration without the victory?" Peggy suggested.

"Chicken!" Cheryl teased.

"I sure am," Peggy answered. "I want to quit while I'm ahead."

Everyone agreed. In a flurry of friendly advice and laughter, Peggy and Ron waved their thanks and stepped out into the chilly evening.

22

A SHARP WIND WHIPPED AT PEGGY'S DRESS. AFTER the warmth of the living room Peggy felt the cold.

Wanting to look dressy, she had chosen a soft wool shawl instead of her coat. That was dumb, she quickly realized. What good will I be as a date if I can't even talk because my teeth are chattering?

"Are you going to be too cold?" Ron asked. "That's not a very warm shawl."

"I'll be okay," Peggy lied. "I'll bet you're cold, too, in just a jacket."

"No, I'm all right."

Peggy started to shiver. She pulled her shawl tighter. Ron noticed.

"I can't do this to you, Peg. Let's go back and phone my mom."

Peggy hesitated. "I hate to." How romantic she thought it would be, strolling home in the nighttime, holding hands and talking. But shivering in the cold, clutching a shawl, trying to outshout the wind—that was only miserable. "I guess maybe we'd better," she conceded.

As they turned back toward Cheryl's place, a car

pulled up. Michael was driving. Darrell opened the back door for them.

"We didn't realize you didn't have a car," Michael apologized.

"Well, on a nice evening it wouldn't be far to walk," Ron replied. "But tonight, even a half block is too far. Thanks for stopping."

Gratefully, Peggy and Ron scrambled into the back seat. "I live on Century Street," Peggy told Michael. "Down near Jeff."

"Oh sure. I know that area," Michael said.

This kills it, Peggy mourned to herself. They'll drop me off and then take Ron home. And I can end the celebration by unlocking my own door and walking in all by myself. And turning out the light. And going to bed. Peggy Marklee's great dating style. Wonderful.

"It's on the left, halfway down the block," Ron told Michael as he turned onto Century. "There, by the streetlight."

"Thanks a lot," Peggy said as they pulled up in front of her place. The bottom was rapidly falling out of her evening.

"We can drop you off, too, Ron, if you want," Michael offered.

"No, no. I live nearby. Thanks, anyhow. This is great."

He knows how to handle things, Peggy sang to herself. The evening could have turned into nothing, but he had saved it.

The car pulled away. Forgetting the cold, Peggy

let her shawl fall from her shoulders as she and Ron raced up the steps.

When she pulled the house key from her pocket, the shawl slipped to the ground. She and Ron almost collided reaching for it. They laughed softly.

"Come on in and get warm," Peggy whispered.

"Is it okay?" Ron whispered back.

"Sure. Why are we whispering?"

They looked at each other and broke out laughing again.

As they closed the door, Mrs. Marklee's head appeared in her bedroom doorway. "Did you have a good time?"

"Wonderful dinner. Wonderful time," Peggy raved.

"Fix some hot chocolate if you're cold. You'll excuse me if I can't leave my book?"

"Of course," Ron answered, trying not to sound relieved. "Don't worry. I won't stay long."

I hope he will, Peggy thought. She beckoned him to follow her into the kitchen. Ron leaned against the counter while she fixed two steaming mugs of cocoa.

"Let's take them in to the couch."

Peggy handed one mug to Ron and picked up the other.

They settled back comfortably, warming their cold hands on the hot mugs.

"This is nice," Ron said. "We don't have many chances just to talk alone, do we?"

Peggy thought back over the tense events that had absorbed them for days. It's time to pay attention to some things that are important to Ron, she realized.

Lately, everything has concerned me. We've got to get back to the closeness we had up on the Point.

"Will your folks let you get your license right on your birthday the way you'd planned?" Peggy asked.

She had chosen the right subject. Ron was instantly alive.

"They said I could take the test the day I turn sixteen," he answered. "And for my birthday present my dad is paying for three months of insurance. After that, I'll have to pay my own insurance costs—and gas, of course."

"Then you'll have to get a job?"

"Yeah. My dad has some contacts with the parks. I'd take even a crummy job just to work out of doors."

Ron grew more excited as he talked about his plans.

"Can your folks get along without their car if you want to borrow it?" Peggy asked.

"It's not hard if they know in advance," Ron told her.

He set his empty cocoa mug on the coffee table. "In fact, I've reserved the car for the whole Saturday following my birthday."

"Oh? What are you planning to do?" Peggy's mind was racing ahead to millions of ways to spend a day in a car.

"Oh, I was going to take an old friend and drive up the coast."

I might have known it, Peggy thought. Her dreams suddenly clouded over. A couple of guys enjoying a car.

"Sounds fun." Peggy tried not to appear disappointed. "Who are you going with?"

Ron was idly shifting the cocoa mug on the coffee table. "I haven't asked the friend yet."

"Oh." Peggy's tone was flat. She didn't really want the details. She tried to think about something else.

Ron took Peggy's mug and placed it beside his.

"Will your mother let you go, Peg?"

Ron didn't seem to know he had just dropped a bombshell. Peggy's heart soared. It's real, she was telling herself. He said it. He asked you a question. Answer him, dummy.

"I'll have a whole month to soften Mom up," Peggy managed to answer. "I'll be there. Count on it!"

Ron raised a fist to pound Peggy's knee as usual. Instead, he reached his arm around her shoulders and pulled her close.

Peggy leaned her hand on Ron's shoulder. His chin rested on her hair.

"You know, Peg, we've been through a lot together. Do you realize that?"

"Uh-huh. I sure do."

"There have been some scary things."

"Uh-huh."

"And some great moments."

"Uh-huh!"

"Quite a lot of activity for a boy from the mountains and a girl from St. Anne's."

"If my friends from St. Anne's only knew," Peggy said dreamily.

"Yeah," Ron answered. "So now, what kinds of things shall we do when we can get our hands on a car?"

Ron's question set off quick flashes in Peggy's mind. Picture after picture. On, off, on, off. A slide show in fast motion. Mossy forest trails . . . sparkling mountain streams . . . grassy meadows . . . pounding surf. Everything. Show me everything, she thought. Show me your whole outdoor world.

"Still there?" Ron asked softly. "I asked you a question. What do you want to do?"

Peggy smiled up at him. "Go fishing."

"Now that," Ron said, bringing his fist down gently on Peggy's knee, "is my kind of girl." He kissed the top of her head.

Now that, Peggy thought smugly, is a girl who is learning.

PHYLLIS ANDERSON WOOD teaches basic reading and writing skills at Jefferson High School in Daly City, near San Francisco. Her students always preview and react to her manuscripts before she considers them ready for publication. A graduate of the University of California at Berkeley, she completed a graduate year in drama and education at Stanford University, and holds an M.A. from San Francisco State University.